THE EDGE

ONE HUNDRED YEARS OF
SCOTTISH MOUNTAINEERING

THE EDGE

ONE HUNDRED YEARS OF
SCOTTISH MOUNTAINEERING

Cameron McNeish & Richard Else

BBC Books

MOUNTAIN SAFETY

Appropriate safety precautions should always be taken when venturing on to the Scottish hills. Don't go without waterproof and spare inner clothing, food, a map, compass, whistle and torch. Scottish winter conditions can often be arctic, and as severe as those on higher European mountains, and should be treated with the utmost respect: an ice axe, crampons and specialist winter gear are essential in winter, as is an understanding of snow conditions, including avalanches and cornices. All venturing on to the Scottish hills in winter should be able to navigate accurately especially as the weather often changes extremely quickly. Scottish climbing courses are offered by numerous qualified instructors and organizations operating in the highlands.

PREVIOUS PAGE: Classic winter mixed climbing for which Scotland is world famous. Jas Hepburn on Scorpion (V), Carn Etchachan, Loch Avon, Cairngorms. A party including Tom Patey made a remarkable first ascent here in 1952.

To the climbers…

Published by BBC Books, a division of BBC Enterprises Limited, Woodlands, 80 Wood Lane, London W12 OTT

First published in 1994

Text © Cameron McNeish and Richard Else 1994
The right of Cameron McNeish and Richard Else to be identified as the Authors of this Work has been asserted by them in accordance with the Copyright, Design and Patents Act 1988.

A Cooling Brown production for BBC Books

Edited by James Harrison
Designed by Sue Rawkins and Arthur Brown

Set in 11/16pt Goudy

Printed and bound in Great Britain by Clays Ltd, St Ives plc
Jacket printed by Belmont Press Ltd, Northampton
Colour separations by Wellmak Ltd, Hong Kong

ISBN 0 563 37084 X

CONTENTS

AUTHORS' PREFACE

This book accompanies the BBC television series of the same name and grew out of a belief that Scottish climbing encompasses a rich heritage and has a dynamic presence today that deserves a wider audience. We are delighted to have an opportunity to develop many of the themes raised in the television programmes and to deal with some aspects that were omitted due to the inevitable constraints of time.

We would like to thank all who climbed for the programmes and who hung in the most precarious positions, often in appalling conditions and sometimes encumbered by period dress, whilst we attempted to capture their contributions on film. We also acknowledge a debt of gratitude to all the climbers who answered our many questions and who provided material for this project. Especial thanks are due to Rab Anderson, Chris Bonington, Martin Boyson, Alistair Cain, Robin Campbell, Ken Crocket (who as current editor of the *Scottish Mountaineering Club Journal* has allowed us to quote extensively from its pages), Andy Cunningham, Dave Cuthbertson, Mark Diggins, Graeme Ettle, Mick Fowler, Allen Fyffe, Joanna George, Alan Kimber, John Lyall, Hamish MacInnes, John MacKenzie Earl of Cromartie, John McLean, Jimmy Marshall, Graham Moss, Bill Murray, Ian Nicholson, Andy Nisbet, Paul Nunn, Clive Rowland, Steve Sustad, Tam the Bam, Mick Tighe and Tom Weir. A number of companies have been generous with their support for our special requests and we would like to acknowledge the valuable assistance given by Berghaus and Cairngorms Ropes.

The films that accompany this book were made by an enthusiastic team and their efforts, especially in the best winter Scotland has seen for years, must not go unrecorded. They were Duncan McCallum (climbing camera), Colin Godfrey (camera), Keith Partridge (sound) and Phil Swainson (runner). Most importantly this project could not have been successful without a safety team expertly led by Brian Hall and including Dave Cuthbertson, Mark Diggins, Alan Kimber, Paul Moores, Mick Tighe and John Whittle. The thanks of the whole team go to Dave Clem, an outstanding pilot and keen climber, who proved on numerous occasions that it was possible to not only dump people on the flimsiest of ledges but also to collect them from such positions!

In the offices of Triple Echo Productions David Taylor (executive producer) and Laura Hill (production manager) succeeded in imposing a measure of order on the natural anarchy of climbing and ensured the smooth progress of an enterprise that relied on flexibility and a shrewd interpretation of Met Office forecasts.

CLIMBERS ON THE BEN NEVIS PLATEAU AFTER COMPLETING WINTER ROUTES.

Thanks are also due to Colin Cameron and Ken MacQuarrie at BBC Scotland without whose insight and faith there would have been neither films nor book; to Suzanne Webber and Khadija Manjlai at BBC Books for calmness in the face of a deadline that would test the resolve of most mountaineers, and to James Harrison, Sue Rawkins and Arthur Brown at Cooling Brown who have proved that computer discs and a mountain of images can be assembled into what, we trust, is a coherent work. Margaret Wicks has earned the gratitude of us both by undertaking much of the research, preparing the manuscript and liaising with the climbers.

Finally we have tried to steer a difficult course between a book that is aimed at those who enjoy the thrill of vertical ground and others who prefer the theory rather than the practice! Inevitably, part of the attraction of Scottish climbing lies in its inherent controversy and the barroom debate that accompanies any discussion of routes or climbers. However, this is hardly comforting news for anyone prepared to commit themselves to print, therefore the responsibility for any mistakes, or of a particular viewpoint, must remain ours.

CAMERON MCNEISH *and* RICHARD ELSE
8th May 1994

7

A CLASSIC SCOTTISH WINTER SCENE:
CREAG AN DUBH LOCH IN THE CAIRNGORMS.

BLUE
REMEMBERED HILLS

Lurg Mhor, in British terms, is a remote mountain. Land-locked away beyond the head of lonely Loch Monar in the northern highlands of Scotland and girdled by trackless miles, it shares with its near neighbour Bidein a'Choire Sheasgaich the reputation of being one of Scotland's most isolated and inaccessible mountains.

Remote too are Seana Braigh in Wester Ross, and A'Mhaighdean and Ruadh Stac Mor in the wild, unpeopled quarter of mountains between Loch Maree and Little Loch Broom. The hills of the Knoydart Peninsula, perched precariously in limbo between the long biting fjords of Loch Nevis and Loch Hourn (whose names in translation from the Gaelic mean the lochs of heaven and hell), are no less inaccessible.

Easier to reach but much harder to climb are the jagged gabbro and basalt peaks of the Black Cuillin on the Isle of Skye, Britain's most Alpine-like mountains. In direct contrast, on the opposite side of the country, the Cairngorms are higher but offer more rounded slopes, thrusting massive plateaus above wind and frost scoured cirques, an area of genuine Arctic tundra offering a home to a herd of reindeer, and flocks of ptarmigan, dotterel and snow buntings, birds more usually associated with the frozen wastes of Iceland, Greenland and northern Scandinavia.

Such is the variety of the Scottish mountains. In European terms these are obviously not high mountains, Ben Nevis, the highest, is only 4409 feet (1344 m) above sea level, but because of their latitude and the often cold and windy weather which their northerly position attracts, these hills offer a very real challenge.

9

There are no glaciers among the Scottish mountains; permanent snow lies only in a couple of odd patches in the higher hills. Most of the tops can be climbed and descended comfortably in a day, but a lack of tracks and trails in open country where mist and rain often reduces visibility can make navigation extremely complex. In winter conditions – any time between November and May – there is a real threat of avalanche, whiteout conditions and full scale Arctic blizzards. Only the foolhardy treat the Scottish hills with anything less than respect.

But the Highland weather, often cursed and yet, because of its complexity and fickleness often misunderstood, can provide the stimulation that only comes from being in an environment enhanced by wreaths of mist or sunlight filtered through a cloud level which, from below, may appear depressing. Many are the occasions when it is a real struggle to leave a warm sleeping bag in a tent or a flickering bothy fire, when the drizzle and cloud seem, at first, impenetrable, only to find that once the mountain is reached you are enjoying it. And how often that mental struggle is rewarded with a clearing of the cloud, even momentarily, like a swiftly raised curtain, over a complete landscape that looks as though it has been newly laundered and hung out to dry, crackling with freshness.

Then there are the days which remain longest in the memory, when the rock is warm to the touch, when every burn is an oasis and every far-flung view shimmers on a haze borne by sun on damp rock and heather. In conditions like this it's easy to understand what motivates climbers. Norman Collie, one of Scotland's pioneering climbers, writing in the *Cairngorm Club Journal*, considers the question of the freedom of the hills,

> Many are the memories one can bring back from the mountains, some of the peace
> and some of the stern fights with the elements, but they are all memories of freedom.
> The restraints of ordinary life no longer holds us down, we are in touch with nature –
> the sky, the winds, the waters, and the earth, surely these ancient elements of life can
> teach us secrets that a more protected existence hides from us. In the old Gaelic lore
> that deals with a people whose daily world lay close to the earth, one sees how their
> passion for freedom is told in their poetry. It came from their intimate relation with
> nature. May we not also find contentment and a larger interest in life from friendly
> communion with the hills and the wide open spaces of our highland land?

It is only comparatively recently that Scotland has been well mapped, and indeed, safe enough to travel through. The Highland Line, a geological and geographical fault

PRINCIPAL CLIMBING AREAS IN SCOTLAND

Far North: *This area was largely ignored by all but a few climbers. In the sixties new routes were put up on mountains like Liathach but in the past decade smaller areas like the Ardmair Crags have been opened up by Scottish enthusiasts.*

Cairngorms: *Ignored by most early climbers, these granite mountains were brought to prominence in the fifties. Led by Tom Patey, Aberdonian climbers explored the numerous untouched corries and crags and soon doubled the existing number of climbs.*

Creag Meagaidh: *Situated between the Cairngorms and Lochaber this mountain has seen new routes put up by climbers as diverse as Harold Raeburn, Jimmy Marshall, Dougal Haston and Tom Patey.*

Ben Nevis: *Britain's highest summit has attracted exploration from the eighteenth century onwards. Collie made the first winter ascent of Tower Ridge, while Raeburn's contribution is reflected in the routes bearing his name.*

Glencoe: *Ideal for demanding winter and summer routes Glencoe, including Bidean nam Bian, has been pivotal in encouraging advances in British climbing. The immediate post war years saw the domination of the Clydeside Creagh Dhu Club but this was soon challenged by climbers from Edinburgh and Aberdeen.*

Arrochar Alps: *Easily accessible from Glasgow it was here that W.H. Murray climbed his first mountain, The Cobbler. Later the area formed a*

convenient base for much of the early activity of the Creagh Dhu and here they developed new techniques brought over from the Continent.

The Cuillin of Skye: *Professor Norman Collie explored and mapped these mountains of Skye and helped to bring their importance to the forefront of the mountaineering world.*

THE NORTH EAST CORRIE OF LOCHNAGAR, SCENE OF MUCH ACTIVITY
BY THE ABERDONIAN SCHOOL OF CLIMBERS AND WHERE TOM PATEY MADE THE FIRST
WINTER ASCENT OF DOUGLAS-GIBSON GULLY IN 1950.

which runs across the country from Loch Lomond to Stonehaven was until the nineteenth century the dividing line which separated what we would call civilization from those who Sir Walter Scott described as 'much addicted to predatory excursions upon their Lowland neighbours'.

Military map-makers like General Roy appeared in the highlands about 1750, followed by the road map-makers, and in 1791 the ordnance surveyors. Next came the scientists, the geologists, the zoologists and botanists, and the social explorers like Thomas Pennant, Dr Samuel Johnson and James Boswell. In the early years of the nineteenth century, J.D. Forbes of Edinburgh, a Professor of Natural Philosophy, travelled widely, climbing mountains throughout the highlands, making the first recorded ascents of Sgurr nan Gillean and Bruach na Frithe on the Isle of Skye. His chief interest was in glaciology, and in 1857 he became the first honorary president of the Alpine Club in London which was founded that year.

However, it was an indigenous Highlander by the name of Sherrif Alexander Nicolson who became Scotland's first mountaineer in the modern sense. Born in Huabost on Skye in 1827, Nicolson studied in Edinburgh and became a prominent lawyer. As a natural explorer, and spending his holidays at home on Skye, he set out to climb Sgurr Alasdair (Gaelic for Peak of Alexander and thus named after him), Sgurr Banachdich and Sgurr Dearg. Later he climbed Sgurr Dubh Mor from Coruisk after walking in from Sligachan.

Yet it was not only the learned and the wealthy who were attracted by mountains. In 1868, Neil Marquis, the son of the local Glencoe shepherd, climbed up the north face of Aonach Dubh above Loch Achtriochtan to reach the long vertical slit of Ossian's cave. It was Glencoe's first recorded rock climb.

Between 1849 and 1875, Scotland saw the formation of several 'outdoor clubs', mostly in Edinburgh and Glasgow, the most prominent being the Cobbler Club, formed in 1866, and the Cairngorm Club in 1888. These clubs were among the first to devote themselves to climbing, rather than general walking and rambling.

It doesn't take much geographical insight to realize that Scotland is a very mountainous country indeed – although in the latter years of the last century it was generally thought that there were perhaps only thirty mountains over the height of 3000 feet (914 m) in the entire nation. But in 1890 a soldier and diplomat by the name of Sir Hugh Munro, of Lindertis in Angus, compiled a list of the 3000-foot mountains of Scotland. The Munros, as they are now known, comprise 277 Scottish mountains which lift their heads over the 3000 foot contour (while the Corbetts make up another 221 separate hills over 2,500 feet [762 m]), and are scattered at random throughout the country.

Following Sir Hugh's listing of his 3000 foot peaks in one of the early *Scottish Mountaineering Club Journals*, it became almost fashionable for club members to climb them, ticking them off carefully. Many of Scotland's early mountaineers found a new challenge on their own doorstep, a challenge which was as satisfying as the Alpine peaks and by no means a 'poor man's substitute'. The *Scottish Mountaineering Club Journal* of 1896 contains the prophetic entry,

Moncrieff and Robertson bagged Beinn Chaluim. Of their adventures nothing is recorded further than that they went up the hill and came down again. As this particular hill exceeds 3000 feet, its ascent therefore comes in the shape of a duty to the conscientious peak-bagger.

Who says Munro-bagging is a new phenomenon? Nevertheless it was ten years after Munro's compilation before anyone completed all the Munros, and this honour fell to the Reverend A.E. Robertson. (Another gentlemen of the cloth, the Reverend A.R.G. Burn, made the second round, twenty two years later.) Robertson was both a good climber and a meticulous planner. His final summit was on the Aonach Eagach ridge in Glencoe, and it is said he kissed the cairn, and his wife, in that order.

In recent years, the Munros have been run, traversed on ski and on mountain bike (carrying the bikes along the vertiginous Cuillin Ridge and Aonach Eagach ridge sounds like purgatory, but each to his own), and have been completed by young and old, male and female. Several dogs have made the round too. Surprisingly, in view of the numbers of people who climb the Munros today, it was not until 1971 that the number of Munroists reached 100. Many hundreds more have become members of that once elite band since and today Munro-bagging has become an accepted part of Scottish mountaineering.

In the two or three decades before Munro's compilation, Scotland boasted a handful of Alpine Club members. This London based club was very much the epicentre of the mountaineering world at the time. It was an association of the gentry and the Scottish members regarded the Scottish hills as a fine training ground for the higher mountains of Europe. One man, William Wilson Naismith, a chartered accountant and insurance manager, felt differently. For him there was a real attraction in climbing Scotland's mountains for their own sake.

In a letter to the *Glasgow Herald* in January 1889 he invited fellow mountaineers to form a 'Scottish Alpine Club', suggesting that,

> The charm of the Swiss mountains is almost beyond description, but a very fair substitute may be found nearer home, namely, by climbing the Grampians in winter or spring. In fine frosty weather such ascents are most enjoyable and afford good practice for subsequent *Scrambles Amongst the Alps*. [This was the title of Edward

Whymper's book, first published in 1871, which included a dramatic account of the first ascent of the Matterhorn in the Valais Alps of Switzerland.] If conducted with ordinary common sense they are free from danger, but the party ought to be provided with hob-nailed boots, a rope, and an ice-axe for cutting steps.

Four days later, a reply appeared in the newspaper from someone who called himself, appropriately, 'Cairn'. This was the joint pseudonym of Gilbert Thomson and D.A. Archie, who, while in favour of forming a club, suggested somewhat harshly,

> The proposal by Mr. Naismith to start a Scottish Alpine Club is one worthy of consideration. The Alpine part is of no present interest, but the Highland one is... .

Naismith responded favourably shortly afterwards, and on 19 January 1889, Ernest Maylard wrote to the paper suggesting the name 'Scottish Mountaineering Club'. On the 11th February a meeting was held in the Christian Institute in Glasgow under the chairmanship of Professor George Ramsay, who had founded the aforementioned fellowship of outdoor lovers called the 'Cobbler Club'. About forty enthusiasts attended that meeting, from which a committee was set up to propose a constitution. As a result of that meeting, the Scottish Mountaineering Club was formally established on 11 March 1889, with a membership of ninety four, several of whom were already members of the Alpine Club. It seems there were no ladies present. Indeed a hundred years elapsed before women were allowed to become members.

Within a very short time of its formation, the Scottish Mountaineering Club became a real driving force, particularly in winter mountaineering. One of its founders, W.W. Naismith, wrote,

> If in the Alps the tide of fashion sets towards rock climbing, to the neglect of snowcraft, those of us with conservative instincts will, by encouraging ascents in snow, have the gratification of helping in some way to stem the prevailing current.

And conservative instincts appeared to be rife within the Victorian fellowship of the SMC. Harold Raeburn, who joined the SMC shortly after its formation, was something of the maverick of his era, exploring rock and ice and leaving routes on many mountains in the highlands. Among his greatest winter achievements were Crowberry Gully on Buachaille Etive Mor in 1893, and, on Ben Nevis, Green Gully in 1906 and Observatory Ridge in 1920. He also made the first summer ascent of Observatory Ridge – solo.

CHRIS FORREST MAKING THE FIRST WINTER ASCENT OF
'WATCHTOWER' (GRADE V), COIRE NA CICHE,
BEINN A'BHUIRD, CAIRNGORMS IN 1986.

Others climbers soon followed Raeburn's example. The exploits of William Hutchison Murray, Mackenzie, Dunn, MacAlpine and Bell, so magnificently and romantically related in *Mountaineering in Scotland* and *Undiscovered Scotland*, inspired generations of climbers to come, but it was in the late forties and early fifties that a new era began. During this time worldwide attention had moved from traditional mountaineering to large scale rock climbing; climbers swarmed up the great cliffs on some of Europe's great mountains and in America the massive walls of Yosemite were being ascended by tension climbing techniques – what climbers later recognized as 'artificial climbing'. These techniques were enthusiastically adopted by Scottish climbers too, particularly the Creagh Dhu club from Clydeside and it's largely because of their contribution that this was the only period in Scotland's mountaineering history when rock climbing development was comparable to that south of the border.

The Scots, considered by the leading Californian climber, Yvon Chouinard, to have formed 'the most vigorous and outrageous backwater of the climbing fraternity', seemed to take delight in being contrary to popular fashion. While the rest of the world concentrated on the athleticism of rockcraft and the technical developments of piton-craft and ironmongery, Scottish climbers continued to take a perverse pleasure in their own brand of extremism – winter mountaineering.

By the sixties the art of front-pointing had been adopted by the Scots when the French crampon manufacturer Grivel added two extra points to the front of their crampons. This allowed climbers to kick into the snow or ice, and step up, using the front points of the crampons for purchase – much less tedious than step cutting and a technique which allowed greater speed and freedom. Together with new ice axe designs and techniques, Scotland saw an avalanche of bold new routes which soon caught the imagination of foreign climbers. It was not long before climbers came north in greater numbers daring to enter the lion's den and to claim some of the plum routes. French, Swiss, German and Americans ventured on to the mixed routes of Glencoe and the Ben, with the great Californian climber Royal Robbins remarking that he visits Scotland every once in a while 'to recharge my ethical batteries'.

At the forefront of this new development was a strong and immensely bold Creagh Dhu climber by the name of John Cunningham. Working at the very limit of ice steepness, Cunningham, along with his regular partner Bill March, both at this time instructors at the Scottish National Sports Centre, Glenmore Lodge, climbed the short, vertical Chancer, on the Hell's Lum Crag which overlooks the remote Loch A'an in the Cairngorms. (In those days the public road stopped at Coylumbridge and the Cairngorms were truly remote.) Using a combination of front pointing techniques and ice daggers, and taking advantage of natural holds in the ice, just as in rock climbing, the pair created this, the first vertical Scottish ice climb to be put up without cutting steps. Cunningham went on to become an absolute master of the craft of snow and ice climbing. His handbook, *Snow and Ice Techniques*, became a best-seller and he showed an incredible aptitude in assimilating and modifying climbing techniques from all around the world to suit Scottish conditions.

At this time all metal-shafted ice axes were being manufactured in Glencoe by Hamish MacInnes and were infinitely stronger than the traditional wooden-shafted axes. While the front pointing techniques meant that ice climbs could be ascended considerably quicker than by cutting footholds, climbers still had to chop out hand-holds. This problem was overcome by the use of two short axes, the picks of which were driven into the ice above the climber's head, and offered a tentative hold, or at least, balance.

But the straight picks of these short axes had the disconcerting habit of coming out of the ice, a fact well noted by the leading climbers of the thirties who had pronounced the technique to be too dangerous and unjustifiable. So the inventive brain of MacInnes tried to find the answer by developing a special curved pick, one with exactly the correct angle so the pick wouldn't pop out of the ice at inopportune moments. In 1970, simultaneous experimentation was going on in America in the workshops of two Californian climbers, Doug Tomkins and Yvon Chouinard. That year the two Americans visited Scotland, bringing with them rigid crampons and a hammer, and an axe, both with curved picks. They raised Scottish eyebrows when they proceeded to knock off one of the ripe plums of the era, the desperate Direct Finish to Raven's Gully in Glencoe.

Chouinard showed his new climbing tools to an Edinburgh climber and gear retailer, Graham Tiso, who, with the sound entrepreneurial judgement which was to eventually make him Britain's most successful outdoor equipment retailer, recognized their potential for serious Scottish ice routes. This was the first of several meetings which were to change the face of winter climbing in Scotland. Tiso was aware of Cunningham's experimentation with ice daggers, and took Chouinard north to meet him at Glenmore Lodge. Cunningham's reputation as a hard climber was well known and Chouinard was duly impressed. Cunningham was equally impressed with the new American ice climbing tools and arranged a meeting with Hamish MacInnes in Glencoe at the Clachaig Inn. It was, in many ways, an historic meeting.

Hamish MacInnes had been experimenting at length with his drop-head tools and curved picks. After examining Chouinard's axes, his own hammer axe, known to all and sundry as 'The Message', was adapted and changed into a weird looking tool with a prehistoric look to it. The pick, while still straight, was inclined downwards at an angle of 55° to its tubular alloy shaft, and even made the American tools look standard. He called it the 'Terrordactyl'. That year, 1970, MacInnes successfully tested the 'Terrordactyl' in the Russian Caucasus and it soon became standard equipment for ice climbers for the next ten to fifteen years.

In the past three or four decades Scotland's contribution to world mountaineering has been considerable, and not just in the area of technical development of winter climbing. A succession of fine Scottish climbers have also written extensively about their sport, following a tradition which goes back beyond the turn of the century. The works of W.H. Murray, Tom Patey, Jimmy Marshall and Robin Smith and many other lesser known climbers have created a library of literature that is out of all proportion to the popularity of the sport, but which has inspired generations of younger climbers even to the present day. One of the very earliest of climbers to leave a fine legacy of Scottish mountain writing was in fact an Englishman, although he considered himself as an 'adopted Scot'. His name was Norman Collie.

PROFESSOR NORMAN COLLIE IN THE CHEMISTRY LABORATORY
AT UNIVERSITY COLLEGE, LONDON.

NORMAN COLLIE:
THE MANCHESTER SCOT

Norman Collie achieved a distinction which only one other Englishman, before or since, has achieved. A Scottish mountain, Sgurr Thormaid (Norman's Peak) on the Skye Cuillin, was named after him. Not so far away along the tight contorted ridge another peak, Sgurr Thearlaich, (Charles' Peak) is named after the Lakeland climber Charles Pilkington.

Although often mistaken as being Scots, J. Norman Collie was born in Manchester in 1859. His father was of Celtic origin – part Scots, part Irish – and his mother Catherine came from a prominent middle-class family – she was one of the five daughters of Henry Winkworth, a silk manufacturer with mills in Manchester. Catherine was a strong willed woman who dedicated much of her life to furthering the education of women and helped to set up a Working Women's College in Manchester. Her brother Stephen was a climber who was later elected to the Alpine Club.

During Norman's early years the family business began to flounder, and the family moved to Scotland in 1865. They stayed at Bridge of Allan for some months before moving north to Glassel House on Deeside where Collie's passion for exploration grew into a deep, abiding love for wild places and wild things. A slim lad with aquiline features, he was shy and taciturn, happy with his own company and with little interest in other people. Nevertheless, like so many reserved people, Norman had a strong sense of family kinship, no doubt developed by his mother's strong family ties. With three brothers and a sister, he was particularly close to his elder brother Henry, with whom he was to share many of his future adventures.

Collie enjoyed those youthful years, exploring the woods and fields which surrounded the lowly Hill of Fare in rural Aberdeenshire. But his mother, strong willed and matriarchal, badly missed her literary friends, her artistic soirées and socialising. She hated living in Scotland, and largely as a result of her insistence, the family moved to Clifton near Bristol to be close to the rest of the Winkworth family, and Collie's days of being footloose and fancy free came to an abrupt end.

He was sent as a boarder to Charterhouse and he loathed it – hating the discipline and the bullying. At one point he even considered drowning himself. But when he was sixteen, the American Civil War seriously affected the price of cotton, and the family's fortunes crumbled. Norman was taken out of his expensive, fee-paying school and sent to Clifton College as a day boy. He did not shine as a student, indeed it was suggested he should leave because he was so bad at classics. Later however, he began to blossom as an academic. At University College, Bristol he studied science under Professor Edmund Letts. In his third year Letts thought so highly of him that he appointed him his paid assistant to accompany him to his new post in Belfast. Collie spent three years in Ireland working closely with Letts and they jointly published two scientific papers.

After studying in Germany for his Ph.D., Collie came home to Britain to take up the position of a teacher at Cheltenham Ladies College, but this was to be another unhappy and unfulfilling period in Collie's life for at this time there was a great prejudice against men teaching girls. But it was also during this interlude, in 1886, that he went on an angling holiday with his brother Henry to the Isle of Skye and it was this vacation that radically changed his life.

Uncharacteristically for the Western Isles, the weather was superb, and the long sunny days were too hot for fishing. Instead they climbed those black gabbro peaks which were to become so familiar in the years to come. It is important to remember that at this time climbing as a sport was very much in its infancy and the whole concept of scrambling your way up a mountain was still a novelty. It was therefore with some surprise that the two brothers were stopped in their tracks by the sight of two climbers high on a crag above them. To Collie, it was a revelation,

> I sat with mountaineers hundreds of feet above me, on what appeared to be rocks as
> steep as the walls of a house. In those days I knew nothing about climbing, and it
> seemed to me perfectly marvellous that human beings should be able to do such things.

That evening, in the Sligachan Inn, Collie sought out and introduced himself to the

PORTRAIT OF NORMAN COLLIE WHO IS BEST REMEMBERED AS
BEING AN OUTSTANDING EXPLORATORY CLIMBER, AND WHO MADE
A NUMBER OF FIRST ASCENTS IN SCOTLAND, AS WELL AS IN THE
CANADIAN ROCKIES AND LOFOTEN ISLANDS.

climbers. He discovered their names were Socke and Parker, and he interrogated them at some length about mountaineering. What equipment did one require, where could you climb, how difficult was the climbing in the Cuillin? He was firmly told that it was vital to use a rope and that climbing without one was dangerous, so next day he telegraphed home for an alpine rope.

It arrived a few days later and was put to immediate use. To the south west of Sligachan, the bare, rocky walls of Coire a'Bhasteir forms an impressive north facing rampart which is clearly seen from Sligachan. Bounded on either side by prominent pointed peaks – the magnificent Sgurr nan Gillean on the left and the lower Sgurr a'Bhasteir on the right – it is dominated by its central peak, Am Basteir (the Executioner) and its distinctive 'tooth'.

With the intention of climbing Sgurr nan Gillean, appropriately called the Peak of the Young Men, the two brothers set out for the corrie, from where they planned to climb onto the ridge, and then onto the summit. They were not successful. The narrow ridge and several rocky 'gendarmes' proved to much for them and after several hours of

Sgurr nan Gillean (the Peak of the Yound Men)
from a glass slide taken by Norman Collie.

scrambling and scrabbling on the face, they gave up and returned to the inn.

Unperturbed, they tried again the next day and spent many more hours trying first to surmount the pinnacles of Sgurr nan Gillean, and finally the peak itself. But for the second time they were defeated chiefly because they were very inexperienced and the peak was somewhat exposed. Acting on some local advice, they successfully climbed the mountain on their third attempt and for Norman Collie, 'mountain climbing became more important to me than fishing'.

A few days later, intoxicated with the heady mixture of mountain ambition, the brothers engaged the help of a local guide, John Mackenzie of Sconser and the three of them climbed Am Basteir, the Executioner. For Norman Collie it was the beginning of a long-standing mountaineering partnership and the genesis of a life-long love affair with the Cuillin.

Collie and Mackenzie climbed together every time Collie visited Skye. On each visit he would immediately contact Mackenzie at Sligachan, and the two would formulate their plans for the holiday. The guide/client relationship quickly grew into a deep friendship. The two men, from such different backgrounds and cultures, were bound together by a common love and appreciation of the hills.

From guiding visitors to local beauty spots, John Mackenzie had quickly progressed to be a first-rate climber, initially with the Pilkington brothers (who made the first ascent of the Inaccessible Pinnacle of Sgurr Dearg in 1880), W.W. Naismith, and later with Collie, with whom he climbed for almost half a century. By the time he had given up climbing the hills because of his age, he had shared a rope with many of those who made significant contributions to the development of British climbing. He was held in such esteem that the Alpine Club, in later years, always sent him a complimentary copy of the *Alpine Journal* – a rare privilege indeed.

The mountaineer, Ben Humble, writing in 1930, describes a meeting with Mackenzie in Sconser, a tiny village on the shore of Loch Sligachan,

> Later that evening we had the good fortune to fall in with John Mackenzie. We had heard of him, for his name appears in all books on Skye. He is the most famous mountain guide in Britain; a man among men, white-bearded, ruddy complexioned and clear of eye, and though over seventy he was, up till a few years ago, leading the way to the mountain tops. He does not climb now, but is still a mighty fisherman. What a grand life Mackenzie has had! He has watched the growth of rock climbing in Skye from its infancy, and was with the parties when many of the peaks were first climbed. He was one of the first to climb the Inaccessible Pinnacle of Sgurr Dearg and it is fitting indeed that Sgurr Mhic Choinnich (Mackenzie's Peak) should perpetuate his memory.

When they first met Collie was twenty eight and Mackenzie thirty one. In later years Collie described him as a lovable, charming and delightful companion. He recognized in the Gael a deep feel for the wild lochs and moors and suggested that as a companion on a long summer day he was perfect. 'There was only one John', he wrote, 'simple-minded, most lovable and without guile.'

Collie remained a bachelor throughout his life, his only regular female companions being his nieces, his mother and his housekeeper. It was suggested by a friend that the only thing to which Collie gave his heart, first and last, was the Isle of Skye. In the 1897 edition of the *Scottish Mountaineering Club Journal* he wrote movingly of this affection,

> ...when the wild Atlantic storms sweep across the mountains; when the streams gather in volume, and the bare rock faces are streaked with the foam of a thousand waterfalls; when the wind shrieks amongst the rock pinnacles, and the sky, loch, and hill-side is one dull grey, the Coolin can be savage and dreary indeed; perhaps the clouds towards evening may break, then the torn masses of vapour, tearing in mad hunt along the ridges, will be lit up by the rays of the sun slowly descending into the western sea, 'robing the gloom with a vesture of diverse colours, of which the threads are purple and scarlet, and the embroideries flame'; and as the light flashes from the black rocks, and the shadows deepen in the corries the superb beauty, the melancholy, the mystery of these mountains of the Isle of Mist will be revealed.

Although Collie was one of the early pioneers of climbing we are fortunate that he has left behind an outstanding body of writing. He also left a remarkable collection of plate-glass slides which vividly illustrate many of his most famous climbs. When Collie died these were deposited in wooden boxes at the Alpine Club in London. Over the years they lay forgotten in a basement room and were only recently re-discovered. The collection is of paramount importance in our understanding of Collie's achievements and forms a comprehensive pictorial record of his mountaineering, his achievements as a scientist, and the social milieu of the times.

During Collie's increasingly frequent visits to Skye, it did not take him long to realize that the Ordnance Survey one-inch to the mile map was wildly inaccurate, despite the fact that it had only been published the year before his first visit. From his earliest climbs he began making his own maps and estimating the heights of the summits. When he started to check these heights by means of an aneroid barometer he was astonished by the results. Not only did they differ from the ordnance survey readings, as he had expected, but they did not even correspond with his own readings taken a few days earlier. There were two possible sources of error – inaccuracy in the instrument or rapidly changing atmospheric pressure. To tackle the first, he constructed

JOHN MACKENZIE (RIGHT) WITH A CLIENT ON THE SUMMIT
OF SGURR NAN GILLEAN LOOKING ACROSS GLEN SLIGACHAN
TO CLACH GLAS AND BLAVEN.

and designed his own portable mercurial barometer, while for the second he devised a system for using the ordnance survey map for a base and keeping to a minimum the time which elapsed between the readings. His survey of the Cuillin established that at least thirteen mountains were over 3000 feet (914 m), and more significantly, that the highest point on the Cuillin Ridge was in fact Sgurr Alasdair and not, as had been thought, the Inaccessible Pinnacle of Sgurr Dearg.

This discovery was made one day after Collie and Mackenzie had climbed Sgurr Dearg, tackling the great basalt prow of the Inaccessible Pinnacle from its short, steep, western side. They found it hard, with Mackenzie taking his boots off and climbing in his stockinged feet to gain more friction on the wet rock. From the summit Collie looked across Coire Lagan to the south and up to the summit of Sgurr Alasdair. It looked higher and impulsively he decided to check it at once.

JOHN MACKENZIE FROM A GLASS SLIDE TAKEN BY COLLIE. MACKENZIE IS
OFTEN SAID TO BE BRITAIN'S FIRST MOUNTAIN GUIDE AND HIS
CLIMBING IN SKYE SPANNED MORE THAN HALF A CENTURY.

The resulting traverse, from Sgurr Dearg around the rim of Coire Lagan to Alasdair is a rough day's mountaineering, even by today's standards. Lowering themselves off the Pinnacle, they crossed the rocky little peak of An Stac before tackling the long, narrow and exceedingly steep-sided ridge of Sgurr Mhic Choinnich (subsequently named after Mackenzie). From this summit a vertical step in the ridge was avoided by a series of exposed ledges on the west face. This route is now known as 'Collie's Ledge'. A scramble over Sgurr Thearlaich followed by a short vertical descent landed them in the gap at the head of the Great Stone Shoot, from which the sharp little summit of Alasdair was quickly climbed. Collie's earlier hunch had been correct and Sgurr Alasdair was found to be higher than the Inaccessible Pinnacle by twenty three feet. Later, in the *Alpine Club Journal*, he described some of the difficulties met on the ridge,

Everything was wrapped in gloom... one seemed cut off entirely from the outer world and the lonely grandeur of the place and the stillness of the night was a thing I have never forgotten. How many mountains we went over and how many feet we climbed it is impossible to say for in many places we traversed backwards and forwards and up and down in our endeavours to overcome the difficulties that we met with on that extraordinary ridge of the Coolin.

Norman Collie's love affair with the Cuillin falls into three distinct periods – the early years between 1886 and 1891 when he was a regular visitor during his vacations; between 1891 and 1904 when, travelling extensively abroad and throughout the mountain areas of Britain, he was unable to spend much time in Skye; and between 1904 and 1942, when he visited the island much more often and after 1939 remained there permanently.

During this first period he made several important climbs, and laid the foundation for some tremendous exploratory climbing in the future. One of the hardest days he had was with Mackenzie following an itinerary which would make all but the strongest modern mountaineers flinch. The pair began at Sligachan and climbed the Bealach na Glaic Moire. From the summit of Sgurr a'Mhaidaidh they traversed eight of the major Cuillin peaks, including the Inaccessible Pinnacle. From here they traversed around Coire Lagan to Sgurr Alasdair before making the long rough descent of Coir 'an Lochain in the dusk to Loch Coruisk. In complete darkness they ascended the Druim nam Ramh on the north side of the loch before dropping down into Harta Corrie for the long walk through Glen Sligachan. They arrived back at the Inn at midnight.

By this time Collie had met up with a number of other climbers, mostly fellow SMC members, and these climbers primarily aimed to scale the peaks by more difficult routes and without using guides. In many ways these pioneers were the last of the 'peak baggers' and among the first climbers who were motivated by the desire to climb new routes.

While Collie was held in respect by many for his Cuillin explorations and his work as a scientist, many others avoided him, and dismissed him as cold and disdainful. Yet, to those he favoured with friendship he offered an unswerving loyalty. He was undoubtedly a man with an extraordinary personality, a charismatic presence and an immense intellect, yet he provoked diverse feelings amongst his contemporaries. Some loved him, but many loathed him. It was said that he could not stand fools and hated small talk, but there was no artificiality about him. He called a spade a spade, and if he

THE CIOCH FROM A GLASS SLIDE TAKEN BY NORMAN
COLLIE. HE DISCOVERED IT IN 1899, BUT IT WAS A
FURTHER SEVEN YEARS BEFORE HE CLIMBED IT.

did not like someone he did not see why he should make any effort with them. Despite his reputation as something of a loner, he was rather fond of dinner parties, although it has been suggested that his fondness was for good food and wine, not his fellow guests.

By this time Collie had become a highly successful scientist whose work spanned the latter years of the nineteenth century and continued right up to the 1930s. He was an outstanding chemist; the inaugural professor of organic chemistry at University College, London and the man responsible for constructing the first neon lamp and who, in another first, applied x-ray photographs for surgical purposes. A brilliant scientific brain often merged with his deep love and appreciation of art, an inclination which was well noted by those around him. A colleague, Sir Herbert Jackson, once commented, 'Collie, I truly believe that you are far more interested in the colours of the discharges than in the striking phenomena you are recording!'

By the 1890s, Collie's reputation as a mountaineer and explorer had spread throughout Britain. He climbed with some of the most famous names of the time including Mummery, Slingsby, Hastings and Herman Woolley and his climbing expeditions took him to Norway, the Alps, the Nanga Parbat area of the Himalaya and to every part of highland Scotland.

It was during this period that he climbed some of his most enduring routes, in particular the first winter ascent of Tower Ridge on Ben Nevis in 1894 with three English companions. Unknown to Collie's party, Tower Ridge had actually been descended two years earlier by the Hopkinson brothers of Keswick. But Collie's ascent of Tower Ridge was very much a winter climb with the Observatory on the summit reporting that the snow was lying more heavily than it had for years, and Collie likening the climb to the Italian Ridge on the Matterhorn. On hearing of Collie's ascent W.W. Naismith wrote, 'the Sassenachs have indeed taken the wind out of our sails most notoriously, I will say that. …Those beggars were more wide-awake then we… Flodden or even Culloden was nothing to this…' Interestingly, the following year Collie joined forces with Naismith to make the first ascent of Castle Ridge, also on the Ben. It seemed on Naismith's part to be a case off, 'if you can't beat 'em, join 'em!'

There is little doubt that Collie climbed much more extensively than we realize, but although he was a talented writer, he appeared to have an aversion to recording his routes in the SMC *Journal*, which began publication in 1889. Although he wrote splendid articles on the hills, and particularly on the delights of his beloved Cuillin, he did not see the point of detailed route descriptions. Exploratory climbing had been his life and this was more important than the technical achievements of climbing. It is also possible that his dislike of publicity was partly a fear of spoiling the solitude and remoteness of the mountains, qualities which he personally cherished and which were very dear to him.

By 1896 news of the potential of new routes on great faces of untouched rock on Skye reached climbers from all parts of the country and Collie found himself joined by other members of the SMC, determined to search out and tackle new climbs. In 1899 Collie made his greatest discovery on Skye. Climbing with Charlie Bruce and Gurkha Harkbir on Sgurr Alasdair, they were returning to Glen Brittle by the lochan in Coire Lagan when Collie noticed that the westering sun was slanting across the face of Sron na Ciche. One great shadow in the middle of the face held his attention for some moments until he suddenly realized that it could only be formed by a huge projecting tower of rock. He hurriedly took a photograph, but seven years passed before he had a chance to return to Coire Lagan. In the meantime no-one else had noticed the phenomenon, showing just how unfrequented these hills were at the turn of the century.

In 1906 he returned and described,

> an interesting tower quite removed from the great rock face, standing out in the most imposing way over the Corrie below. From the top to the bottom is at least 1000 feet, perpendicular in many places and a narrow knife edge of rock about 100 feet long runs out from it rather less than half-way down. On each side of the knife edge are steep, clean slabs of rock that at their base overhang the gullies below. At the end of this knife edge is placed the tower that casts its shadow across the great slab. I do not know of any great mass of rock like it in Great Britain. It is not part of the rock face, but stands away from it and its face has a sheer drop of about 500 feet into the corrie below...

Collie christened the great face Sron na Ciche and Mackenzie called the huge tower of rock the Cioch.

> As it turned out it was a climb full of excitement, for one never knew what was around the next corner. We traversed slabs, we worked up cracks, and went right away from the Cioch into the gully on the east side, losing sight of the Cioch altogether. Then we fortunately found a queer traverse unlike any traverse I have ever seen, that led out of the gully across the perpendicular face of the cliff, and back in the direction of the Cioch. But the Cioch itself we could not see, until having got round several corners, suddenly it came into view and we found ourselves on the end of the knife edge. We sat down on that knife-edge, and slowly made our way to the great rock tower at its end, up this we climbed, and John and I were mightily pleased

Photograph: Cameron McNeish.

AM BUACHAILLE, THE 197 FEET (60 M) SEA STACK OFF THE COAST
OF SUTHERLAND, FIRST CLIMBED BY TOM PATEY, JOHN CLEARE
AND IAN CLOUGH IN 1967.

COIRE AN T-SNEACHDA, NORTHERN CORRIES, CAIRNGORMS WHERE MANY
OF THE BOLDEST NEW WINTER MIXED ROUTES HAVE BEEN PUT UP. ALLADIN
BUTTRESS IS PROMINENT AND IT IS HERE THAT THE ROUTE, WHITE MAGIC,
WAS CLIMBED FOR THE SERIES BY RAB ANDERSON AND GRAEME ETTLE.

PHOTOGRAPH: RICHARD ELSE

Photographs: John Whittle, *far right*: Brian Hall

ABOVE: APPROACHING THE GREAT TOWER
ON BEN NEVIS.

RIGHT: MEGA ROUTE X, CENTRAL TRIDENT
BUTTRESS, BEN NEVIS. A 200 FEET (61 M) GRADE V
VERTICAL ICE FALL. DAVE CUTHBERTSON IS LEADING
THE FIRST PITCH.

Walking off the summit of Ben Nevis at sunset
after completing Tower Ridge. Murray's description:
'While we walked slowly off the plateau, it became very
clear to me that only the true self, which transcends
the personal, lays claim to immortality.'

Photograph: Keith Partridge

Photograph: Keith Partridge

TRIPLE ECHO, SGURR A' CHAORACHAIN, APPLECROSS. A FIRST ASCENT OF THIS
ICE-FALL WAS MADE FOR THE SERIES BY MICK FOWLER AND STEVE SUSTAD.

with our climb. After that everyone at Glen Brittle had to climb it and I believe that during that July and August John and I made the first ten ascents of the Cioch.

Within two years there were five different routes up Sron na Ciche – three of them pioneered by Collie. Collie's reticence to discuss his routes was highlighted in August 1906, a month after Collie and Mackenzie had first climbed the Cioch. Two of the prominent mountaineers of the time, H.G. Buckle and G. Barlow arrived in Skye and thought they were making the first ascent of the Cioch via the Cioch Gully and East Gully. They were very surprised to come upon a cairn on the way up the route! That evening in Glen Brittle they wanted to ask Collie what he knew of the route but Collie remained characteristically aloof and unapproachable. Neither man mentioned their climb. It was not until the next year that Barlow received details of Collie's ascent and it wasn't until 1923 that he managed to obtain exact details of the route.

It was the same sense of exploration that saw Collie embark for Canada in 1897. This was the first of five visits that occupied the next fourteen years of his life. At the time of this first expedition large areas of the country were still unmapped and there was only the most rudimentary knowledge from previous explorers. This was a landscape where whole mountain areas were unexplored; at this time the Rocky mountains were as virgin as the Himalaya. There were, as yet, undiscovered ice fields and the height of many of the peaks was not accurately recorded.

For a man who once declared that 'the call of the wilds was stronger than the love of climbing mountains', Collie's climbing in Canada is characterized by an unrivalled list of first ascents, a total of over twenty peaks including Lefroy, Victoria, Gordon, Sarbach, Athabasca, Murchison, Freshfield, Forbes and Neptuak. His achievement is unique and not simply confined to summit bagging; he surveyed a 3000 square mile (7800 sq km) wilderness; calculated the height of many peaks and discovered areas ranging from the Columbia ice field to the Bush Pass. Collie's achievements are even more remarkable when you consider that for most of his time in Canada even the journey to the mountains was utterly exhausting and on these early trips it took days to cover only a few miles with all the dense vegetation being cleared by hand. These journeys were extremely arduous, but when the mountain was finally reached, a successful first ascent brought rewards that few climbers ever have the privilege of experiencing,

> The evening light was one that does not often fall to the lot of modern mountaineers.
> A new world was spread at our feet; to the westward stretched a vast ice-field
> probably never before seen by human eye, and surrounded by entirely unknown,
> unnamed and unclimbed peaks.

Collie was witness to a unique period in Canada's history. He saw an area that, largely through the efforts of the Canadian Pacific Railroad, was developed from a physically demanding wilderness to a tourist attraction designed to rival the Alps. By the time of Collie's later visits it was possible to hire Swiss guides in the railroad's employ and to travel on easy trails to ascend the mountains. Not surprisingly, these new developments rankled Collie (though he was not averse to using the Railroad himself to get to the peaks he wanted to be the first there) and later trips became fraught with rivalry. Collie always thought of himself as an amateur climber and was furious to discover that the Railroad had invited Edward Whymper to Canada. He considered the veteran of the Matterhorn to be a professional mountaineer who had been enticed over from Britain in order to boost business and attract publicity,

> He will simply go and gobble up the whole lot. As a hunting ground for amateurs the
> country was big enough and to spare, but when a professional team lets himself loose –
> well all I can say is damn the man! Why I am so mad about it is that it is not done for
> sport at all or because Whymper has any real liking for the hills. From the beginning
> to end it is dollars.

In the event Whymper was past his peak as a climber, rarely ventured far from the railroad, and achieved little in the country. However, climbing was undergoing a fundamental change and Collie had to agree to climbing Mt. Forbes with the Reverend James Outram. Forbes had long been a cherished goal but his ascent with the mountaineering parson was pure convenience because Collie despised this late-comer for his naked ambition in claiming first ascents of peaks discovered by others.

After his last visit to Canada in 1911, Collie devoted progressively more time to the Isle of Skye and virtually every summer from 1912 he shared a house at Glen Brittle under the shadow of the Cuillin's imposing jagged peaks, with his friend, the artist, Colin Philip.

It is said, quite correctly, that you can stand on the summit of Sgurr nan Gillean and see Collie's climbing achievements in the chain of rocks curving around to distant Gars-Bheinn; nearly all these climbs were undertaken with his life-long friend John Mackenzie and when the latter died in 1933 Collie, aged seventy four but still active, walked alone to the summit of Am Basteir and declared that this would be his last climb. The man who disliked recording detailed routes because they read 'like railways timetables' and 'stripped the mountains of their mystery', nonetheless left a wealth of inspirational writing that served as a template for mountain literature.

At the outbreak of the Second World War, Collie was an isolated and taciturn figure haunting the Sligachan Inn; a new order was beginning with climbers seeking out the clouded Isle and, in doing so, bringing to a close the golden age of exploratory climbing. A young RAF pilot on sick leave, Richard Hillary, was one of the last to see Collie alive and noted in his diary,

> We were alone in the inn, save for one old man who had returned there to die. His hair was white but his face and bearing were still those of a great mountaineer, though he must have been a great age. He never spoke, but appeared regularly at meals to take his place at a table, tight-pressed against the windows, alone with his wine and memories.

Norman Collie died in Skye in 1942 and was laid to rest in a tiny burial ground near Sligachan alongside his dearest and closest friend John Mackenzie of Sconser. The memory of both pioneers lives on in the Cuillin in two peaks which stand firmly astride the narrow, winding ridge, Sgurr Thormaid and Sgurr Mhic Choinnich. Norman's Peak and Mackenzie's Peak are testimony to two men of different cultures, bound together in their common love of these magnificent mountains of the Isle of Skye.

HAROLD RAEBURN IN 1905.

HAROLD RAEBURN: THE 'COMPLEAT' MOUNTAINEER

Harold Raeburn in his book, *Mountaineering Art*, published in 1920, described how, at a comparatively early stage of its existence, the Alpine Club was persuaded,

> …perhaps by the occurrence of some accidents, perhaps by the publication of a book of guideless climbing, perhaps by a 'middle-aged feeling' on the part of some of its then leading members, to put a ban of guideless climbing… I cannot help thinking that those members of the Alpine Club responsible for this attitude, however high and admirable might have been their motives, displayed a great lack both of wisdom and foresight.

Earlier in the 1890s climbers like Mummery, Collie, Hastings and Slingsby proved that British enterprise was neither middle aged nor decadent. For climbers like these showed the world that they were not merely equal, but were often superior to the best of the Swiss guides.

Harold Raeburn, son of an Edinburgh brewer and a member of a fast expanding middle class, was certainly in that superior mould. On his very first outing with the SMC in 1896 he was involved in the first ascent of the Direct Route of the Douglas Boulder at the foot of Tower Ridge, with W. Brown, L. Hinxman and W. Douglas.

Douglas and Brown, along with Tough, Naismith and Collie, were the leading lights of the SMC at that time, making history by taking bold initiatives almost every

HAROLD RAEBURN CLIMBING SALISBURY CRAGS,
EDINBURGH, FEBRUARY 1920.

time they climbed. Raeburn was a guest on that Ben Nevis meet but he had made his mark and was invited by Tough and Brown on an attempt to climb the Centre Post of Creag Meagaidh, a 1300 foot (400 m) snow and ice gully above Coire Ardair, on this great 3707 foot (1130 m) mountain lying between Ben Nevis and the Cairngorms. Their ambitious plan was eventually thwarted by avalanches but it is an indication of the confidence of these early climbers that Centre Post was not climbed until Jimmy Bell finally led the route in March 1937, forty one years later.

At the turn of the century, the ascent of ridges, buttresses and gullies in snow and ice conditions was fast becoming the cornerstone of Scottish climbing. Originally seen as a form of Alpine training, Scottish climbing was increasingly being recognized as a mainstream mountaineering objective, offering big, serious routes over 1000 foot (300 m) in length. At the same time, high standards of rock climbing were being achieved on the warmer, more benevolent crags of England and these new techniques were migrating north of the border, brought by such individuals as the Abraham brothers. In 1900 the Abrahams took a direct line up Crowberry Ridge on Buachaille Etive Mor, straightening out the original route which had been climbed four years earlier by Naismith and Douglas. George Abraham led the difficult 'crux' section of the climb: a committing move (one that progresses upwards with the real danger of no retreat) on small holds onto the exposed face, where he had to balance on sloping holds to gain a scoop in the rock above. This was a totally new way to climb. It relied on friction from the soles of your boots against the rock, good balance, and an unheard of co-ordi-nation between hand and eye. Gone were the days of sheer muscle power – this was del-icate, acrobatic climbing, and the Scottish Mountaineering Club did not like it at all.

For them it was unjustifiable so they left out any mention of the new Direct Route of Crowberry Ridge in that year's SMC *Journal*. Harold Raeburn, by that time a member of the SMC, showed what he thought of this decadent view. He climbed the second ascent a short time later. Raeburn believed that the rock climbing standards which were being established in England and Wales could equally be achieved on his native Scottish mountain crags, and during the next two years he enforced his viewpoint by embarking on a succession of first ascents which pushed up the standards of Scottish climbing as no-one had done before – much to the chagrin of some of his fellow club members. Raeburn's own significant contribution to Scottish mountaineering was a personal drive to push back the known frontiers of possibility. He was to achieve stan-dards previously undreamt of, and he set about it with a determination which bordered on the obsessive.

Following his repeat of the Crowberry Ridge route, he climbed Observatory Ridge and Observatory Face on Ben Nevis, and the very difficult Raeburn's Arete on Nevis's North East Buttress. It was almost as though he was making a personal statement to the SMC cognoscente. It was a Victorian mountaineering equivalent of a two-finger salute – especially when he climbed Observatory Ridge solo.

In reality climbing solo was probably no more dangerous than climbing with a companion. Rope lengths were absurdly short, and the leader had no running protection. Run-outs were very long and the golden rule was a very simple one: the leader must not fall. Generally speaking, they did not.

But having said that, Observatory Ridge of Ben Nevis is a long, serious 1400 foot (420 m) slender route which is climbed by slabs and walls, buttresses, and a system of cracks and grooves to gain the crest of the ridge which then rises to the summit plateau.

Three months earlier, Raeburn, Douglas, Rennie and Ling made a very ambitious winter attempt on the unclimbed Observatory Buttress – the huge wall which looks out on Tower Ridge across the depths of Observatory Gully. Conditions were horrific with the wind blowing spindrift across the ice-glazed rocks, and the team decided to retreat fairly early on. It is interesting to note that this winter route was not climbed until March 1974 when it was given a Grade V, an indication of the confidence and the ability of these Victorian climbers.

Ken Crocket, in his book on Ben Nevis, suggests that as the party retreated from the summit their eyes, 'and those of Raeburn in particular, must have rested often on the next ridge to the east, Observatory Ridge, which was to be the scene of a remarkable solo ascent two months later'. Raeburn had planned to meet SMC members Dr Inglis Clark and his wife Jane, who were often his climbing companions, and who this time were spending several nights at the small hotel which then existed on the summit. He caught an early train and arrived in Fort William at 10 a.m., and then set out to walk up to Coire Leis and the foot of Observatory Ridge. Later, in the SMC *Journal* he wrote,

> I remember three distinctly good bits on it. First the slabby rocks near the foot. Then
> a few hundred feet up an excellent hand traverse presents itself. It is begun by getting
> the hand into a first-rate crack on the left, then toe-scraping along a wall till the body
> can be hoisted on to a narrow overhung ledge above. This does permit of standing up,
> but a short crawl to the right finished the difficulty... The third difficulty, and the one
> which cost the most time, is rather more than half-way up, where a very steep tower
> spans the ridge. I tried directly up the face, but judged it somewhat risky, and
> prospecting to the right, discovered a route which after a little pressure 'went'.

Raeburn took only three hours to climb the 900 foot (270 m) rocky crest, and did not seem to rate it of any great consequence, describing it as a most enjoyable scramble. His ornithological senses appeared to be more impressed on hearing the summer song of the cock snow bunting and he concluded the account of his climb by admitting that if asked to choose between the climb and the song, he would be tempted to choose the song.

The following year the Inglis Clarks were again involved in another of Raeburn's solo epics, this time as distant spectators. Raeburn had been taking part in a yachting race (he was a keen yachtsman in addition to being a climber and an excellent ornithologist), and the Inglis Clarks had previously arranged to meet up with Raeburn at the foot of Observatory Buttress at 2 p.m. Unfortunately, their morning climb, Pinnacle Buttress, had taken them longer than planned, and they only arrived at the top of the Great Tower at 4.15 p.m. Looking down they spotted the moving figure of Raeburn on the rocks of Observatory Buttress. He had grown weary of waiting for his friends and, deciding not to waste the day had climbed the 700 foot (213 m) route solo.

Later, he explained his decision to climb the route in this way,

> Below, was the fast flowing shadowtide; above, the blaze of sunlight, and oh, blessed thought, perhaps afternoon tea. It was enough, I went up, and, fifteen hours from the Sea, stood upon the Summit.

A few days later he climbed a very steep arete formed by the north and east faces of the North East Buttress. This time he climbed in the company of Mr and Mrs Inglis Clark, following a series of steep, parallel ramps. The route was named simply Raeburn's Arete, and he commented briefly that it ranked amongst the steepest on Ben Nevis. Today the route is given a Severe grading.

There is sometimes a temptation to consider Raeburn as a very athletic climber who was far ahead of his time, lacking perhaps the altruistic aestheticism of his contemporaries. But, despite his own apparent dismissal of many of his routes, he was passionately fond of sea and mountains and extremely sensitive to the evocative nature of wild places. In his only book, *Mountaineering Art*, he wrote,

> The mountains, like the oceans, have always been the home of the marvellous and the terrible from the earliest dawn of history. Man, in the main, was and still is, an inhabitant of the flat, and fat, places of the earth. The mountains, with their mysterious, inaccessible white pinnacles, behind which rose and set the sun, were the regions where he could hardly help placing the homes of his earliest Gods. These were the powers of Nature made manifest.

His great friend and climbing partner, William Ling, described Raeburn as a man with an intense love of nature in all its aspects – birds and beasts, flowers and rocks. He spent much of his time climbing sea-cliffs and his diaries on the sea birds of the Shetland Isles contain so much fascinating information that they are lodged with the National Library of Scotland.

While Raeburn was undoubtedly *the* climber of his time, on both snow and rock, he continuously maintained that rock climbing, while perhaps not 'the whole of mountaineering' was a very important part of it. At this time some writers were suggesting that British rock climbing could not be considered 'true mountaineering', but Raeburn maintained that if combined with practice in winter hill-walking and snow-climbing, the British trained mountaineer fully deserved that title, and need fear no difficulties likely to be encountered on any mountain range in the world.

In 1920 he wrote,

> The tendency is rather to over emphasise the importance of difficult rock climbing ability. The author is not a partisan of rocks, or of snow and ice. I think the mountaineer, to be compleat should be perfectly at home on both. There is this to be said about rock-climbing, however. In my opinion, to be a real expert rock climber, on all formations, requires more science, practice, and brains than is necessary for the less varied and less complicated structure of frozen water.

One wonders how much of this belief was established earlier in his career when he attempted The Chasm, high above Glen Etive on Buachaille Etive Mor. His companion was Willie Ling. It was April, and although both climbers were aware that this particular route would be best climbed in dry, summer conditions, the call of the Alps was strong during those months of high summer, so that Scottish climbing tended to be reserved for the winter and spring months. Despite the fact that the route was still choked with old snow, the pair put up a tremendous performance, sometimes climbing in their stocking soles to try and get some adhesion against the slippery, greasy rock surface. In other places the snow was a positive assistance, as it was stacked up against the gully walls effectively reducing the height of some of the pitches. Finally, they were driven out on to the south wall at a point where the last pitch appeared as a slimy, black slit of smooth rock, running with water, high above them.

By this time Harold Raeburn was the dominant force in Scottish climbing, and two of his ice climbs of this time stand out above all others: Green Gully on Ben Nevis and

Buachaille Etive Mor's Crowberry Gully, which he climbed at Easter 1909. These climbs were believed to be so far ahead of their time that they went unrepeated for more than a quarter of a century. It was thirty one years before Green Gully was climbed again, this time by J.H.B. Bell, who was unaware the route had already been climbed. Raeburn's ascent was still unrecognized, and it was not until the 1970s that a real awareness of his contributions have come to light. Likewise, Crowberry Gully was not climbed again for twenty seven years. W.H. Murray, in his book *Scotland's Mountains*, blames Raeburn's own 'sketchy accounts' for the oversights, saying that his route descriptions were inadequate for comparison with other climbs.

But these 'sketchy accounts' contradict other assessments of Raeburn's character, which suggest that he was as methodical in the recording of detail, as he was in his collection of data on sea-birds. Writing in an *SMC Journal* of the time, Lord Mackay, a contemporary of Raeburn's recalled that,

> In controversies as to routes or as to times required, he was a stern opponent. His
> notes of recorded times in every climb achieved, and his constant comparisons by
> small seconds with the time of to-day, were often anathema to me, who preferred to
> enjoy the hopes and the passing incidents at large, without being checked by the
> watch... Something, I sometimes thought, of Stalin was in his make-up. Ever you
> could see his mind, acting as Molotov's, as it came back and back to its original
> assertions. And yet he was ultimately fair in debate.

The ascent of Green Gully marked the high point of Raeburn's career in Scotland. At this time the development of climbing was severely hampered by the available equipment; tweeds offered limited protection against the vagaries of the Arctic conditions and boots were basic, with hobs and clinkers the only nails. Ice-axes tended to be heavy and often too long whilst ropes were too short. The first Golden Age of Scottish climbing was beginning to fade, and in the next few years the events leading up to the Great War took the minds of young men and mountaineers to more serious matters.

No matter how hard he tried, Raeburn could not join up for the war. At forty nine he was considered too old. Many young mountaineers enlisted, and many died, including Charles Inglis Clark, the son of Raeburn's old friends and climbing companions. After the war, Raeburn made what was probably his greatest climb in Scotland, the first winter ascent of Observatory Ridge, on Ben Nevis. With W.A.

Mounsey and F.S. Goggs, the fifty-five year-old Raeburn led all the way in an incredible demonstration of serious, mixed climbing and produced a route which formed a bridge into the next generation.

Raeburn was as radical in his climbing abroad as he was at home. In 1910, along with Willie Ling, he had made the first ascent of the North Face of the Disgrazia and in the same year he made the first solo traverse of the Meije in the Alps. He climbed new routes in Norway and in the Caucasus and in 1920 took part in an expedition to

A PANORAMIC VIEW OF THE NORTH EAST FACE OF BEN NEVIS TAKEN AROUND THE TURN OF THE CENTURY. THE TWO PROMINENT RIDGES ON THE LEFT ARE THE NORTH EAST BUTTRESS AND TOWER RIDGE. SANDWICHED BETWEEN THE TWO ARE OBSERVATORY RIDGE AND OBSERVATORY BUTTRESS. RAEBURN MADE THE FIRST ASCENT OF OBSERVATORY RIDGE, SOLO, IN 1901 AND THE FIRST ASCENT OF OBSERVATORY BUTTRESS, AGAIN SOLO, A YEAR LATER IN 1902.

Kanchenjunga in the Himalayas. A year later Raeburn was chosen leader of an Everest Reconnaissance expedition. Illness overtook him but he still managed to reach a height of 22 000 feet (6705 m) on the mountain, an incredible achievement by a man of his age who was far from well. After the Everest expedition, illness and overwork began to take their toll, and declining health led to his death on 21 December 1926.

Harold Raeburn was one of the true greats of Scottish mountaineering and a measure of the man can be recognized in the fact that between 1896 and 1921 exactly half the new routes climbed on Ben Nevis were his.

Raeburn's total dominance of Scottish climbing has never been repeated and with his death mountaineering in Scotland went into a serious decline. The Great War had taken its toll amongst Britain's male population with a whole generation virtually wiped out, and those who survived had little inclination to endure the long, hard days which were necessary to combat the rock, snow and ice of Scotland's mountains. To all appearance, climbing in Scotland in the 1920s was dead.

TOWER RIDGE, BEN NEVIS: THE LONGEST ROUTE
ON BRITAIN'S HIGHEST MOUNTAIN.

CHAPTER FOUR:

W.H. MURRAY AT EIGHTY: SETBACKS, SUCCESS AND SPIRITUALITY

The Allies' North Africa campaign in 1942 was going horribly wrong. For days on end the Scots had been fighting a rearguard action, pressed back by the tanks of Rommel's 15th Panzer division. No amount of fire power seemed to have any effect on the inexorable progress of the German tanks. They came on, twenty abreast, and even though they were steadily being hit with each shot, the shells just flinched off them in a shower of sparks – blues, reds and yellows. Although the shells could not penetrate the tanks' armour they made them glow red-hot and gave the appearance a devilish advance in the dusk of the desert night.

In an area with very little protective cover, the Scots found a slit trench and dropped into it. This discovery was timely, as the Germans opened fire, machine gunning the ground around them in a deadly, raking fashion. Suddenly, the gunfire stopped, and one of the Scots soldiers, a Captain, tentatively looked over the edge of the trench to see a German commander climb down from his tank and walk towards him waving a pistol in his hand.

The Captain, convinced the commander was going to shoot him in a release of tension, was astonished when the German instead spoke in perfect English, and asked him if he was not feeling the cold of the desert night. Without thinking, the Captain replied nervously, 'It's as cold as a mountain top'. The effect of his answer was dramatic. 'Good God, are you a climber?', asked the German. The German was an keen moun-taineer, but little did he know that the soldier he was taking captive was one of

47

Scotland's finest climbers, a man who was shortly to create a book of mountain memories which would inspire successive generations of British mountaineers. During the years leading up to the outbreak of the Second World War, William Hutchison Murray – more familiarly known as W.H. Murray – had spearheaded a small band who led the renaissance of severe Scottish winter climbing.

It was not until the thirties that the standards set by Harold Raeburn and his contemporaries began to be regained. In 1929 the Scottish Mountaineering Club built a hut high in Coire Leis, just below the great crags, buttresses and ridges of Ben Nevis. They called it the 'Charles Inglis Clark Memorial Hut', in memory of one of their popular younger members who been lost during the Great War and the son of William Inglis Clark, who had climbed so much with Raeburn. This hut led to a new wave of exploration on Ben Nevis and, although this was mainly based around rock climbing, its main activists, G.G. Macphee and Dr J.H.B. Bell, were also closely involved in the resurrection of winter climbing.

The SMC also began to publish climbing guide books, and their early guides to the Cairngorms, Skye and Ben Nevis inspired much development, particularly in the Cairngorms where the 1928 guide contained only a handful of routes on Lochnagar and stimulated members of the Cairngorm Club into adding a dozen more before 1940.

It was against this background that the mountaineering career of the young W.H. Murray was launched. Bill had accidentally overheard a conversation between two people and was mesmerized by their discussion of a climb in Wester Ross. They described a narrow rocky ridge which they were strolling along when the clouds suddenly cleared away to reveal a vista of sea and mountains. It had never occurred to Murray that here was a whole new world of which he knew nothing, a world which was apparently quite accessible and close at hand. He decided to investigate it.

The only mountain he had heard of was the Cobbler, that surrealist looking triple-peaked hill which lies just north of Arrochar, so he went there, in ordinary walking shoes, flannel trousers and a tweed jacket. To his horror, he found the mountain covered in snow, but he carried on, soon finding himself on hard and icy conditions in the corrie which leads to the ridge between the main top and the south peak. He was frightened by the ice and the exposure, but continued to the top where his trepidation melted away as he gazed over a panorama of hills and mountains spread before him like a white topped sea. In his own words, he was 'hooked for life'.

J.H.B. BELL: AN OUTSTANDING CLIMBER DESCRIBED BY
MURRAY AS BEING THE TOUGHEST YET THE KINDEST
CHARACTER HE HAD MET.

On leaving school, Bill became a trainee banker. It was a surprising choice of a career – he was good at English at school, and even at that early stage in his life he wanted to be a writer, but his maths were terrible. However, he passed the entrance exams and at least had the security of a good job in days when those in work were considered to be extremely fortunate. He began going to the hills every weekend, initially on public transport but soon progressing to a Norton 500 motor bike before becoming the proud owner of an Austin Seven motor car. The growing availability of motor cars and increased leisure (often enforced), made the mountains accessible to a new generation of climbers and for the first time, to others than the professional classes.

During the depression of the early thirties, many young men escaped the frustration and boredom of the dole queue of Clydeside and found a new challenge on the rock of the highlands. Often they would walk from their Glasgow homes to the mountains, but as more and more cars appeared on the roads they became expert hitch hikers, turning that age old form of transport into something of an art form. It was at this time that the fairly affluent membership of the SMC became known as the SMT – the Scottish Mountaineering Transport – as climbing partners were sought not so much for their climbing skill, but for their access to motor cars.

While many of these working class pioneers were happy enough to sleep in caves, or howffs, or in ex-army tents, W.H. Murray and his companions had the wherewithal to enjoy the luxury of hotels. The Clachaig Inn in Glencoe, for example, cost five shillings (around seven pounds at today's value) for supper, bed and breakfast. The Inverarnon Hotel at the head of Loch Lomond, or the Kingshouse Hotel in the shadow of the Buachaille Etive Mor were about ten shillings for supper bed and breakfast. When hotels were not available, Murray was affluent enough to be able to buy a high altitude tent which he used to good effect, camping on the high tops within striking distance of the rocks.

It was another golden age in Scottish mountaineering, almost an action replay of the earlier years when exploration of new climbs was a fundamental motivation. These climbers of the thirties enjoyed the mountains for their own sake, climbing new routes when they spotted one, but not particularly searching out new lines. There was an abundance of unclimbed rock so that they were pioneering without actually realizing it.

After a year or so of climbing on his own, visiting the mountains of the Trossachs, the Crianlarich area, the Cairngorms and Torridon, Murray became a member of the Junior Mountaineering Club of Scotland (Junior, because it had less authority than the SMC rather than any upper age limit). Formed in 1925, the club was open to all men aged over seventeen and, unlike the senior SMC, did not require mountaineering qualifications.

It soon became apparent that the best climbers of the JMCS were outshining those of the senior club. There was a tendency for the SMC members (with the exception of Bell, Macphee and some others) to root themselves firmly in the past, and some friction was evident between the two clubs. The qualification for entry to the senior club was, at that time, forty ascents, each ascent being a 3000 foot (914 m) mountain or a climb involving some little difficulty, and by the mid-thirties the JMCS were supplying the SMC with about two thirds of their new members. Ken Crocket, in *Ben Nevis, Britain's*

Highest Mountain, quotes an extract from the Charles Inglis Clark Memorial Hut logbook. This is the book in which climbers would describe their activities on their return from a climb, and the barely disguised barbed comments in this extract disclose something of the uneasy truce which existed between the two clubs in the 1930s,

> April 4th 1937. W.M. MacKenzie, W.H. Murray, A.M. MacAlpine. Gardyloo Gully + arete to Carn Mor Dearg. The gully was found to be ridiculously easy and is not at present recommended to other than complete novices in snow climbing.

Below that entry was written, in another pen,

> This party should try the climb again when there is less, or better still, no snow in the gully. G.G.M.

Not to be outdone, another note followed that,

> The above party has every intention of climbing the gully again under better conditions. They are not unaware that gully climbs vary enormously in winter. On 4/4/37 Gardyloo Gully was easy. W.H.M.

Murray's main climbing companions at that time were Bill Mackenzie, Kenneth Dunn, Archie MacAlpine and, despite being a member of the SMC, Dr Jimmy Bell. Murray described Bell as being the toughest, yet the kindest, character he had ever met in his life. Small and heavily built, Dr J.H.B. Bell hailed from Auchtermuchty in Fife, a son of the manse. He was an industrial chemist by profession and was one of the most brilliant climbers of his generation. It has also been said that Bell's writing ranks beside that of Murray as the most influential of the period.

Perhaps the best route the two climbed together was Parallel Buttress on Lochnagar in 1939. This 900 foot (280 m) rock route is described today as a pleasant route in dry conditions, but the amount of vegetation on it makes it very awkward in wet weather. On that first ascent Bell used a piton driven into a crack in the rocks – first of all as a handhold, then as a foothold. This technique was frowned upon by the climbing establishment of the time and news of this 'aid' created quite a stir within the Scottish Mountaineering Club establishment.

Murray's other significant climbs include the first ascent of the Upper Couloir of Stob Gabhar in the Black Mount, and the first ascent of Clachaig Gully in Glencoe which he climbed in May 1938 with Mackenzie, Dunn and W.G. Marskell. Clachaig Gully had been a challenge to rock climbers ever since Norman Collie led the first party in 1894. It is a long, dank, and more often than not, atrociously wet gully which slits the west face of Sgorr nam Fiannaidh in Glencoe for almost 2000 feet (600 m). Murray himself described the lower sections of the route as, 'like a slice out of Central Africa... climbing up good rock through exotic jungle scenery,' but the trees, the vegetation and the crashing torrents are soon passed as the bare rock walls of the gully rise gradually on either side. Higher up, the route necessitates a good drenching. In Murray's own words,

> I edged cautiously round the pool through hissing spray, hesitated, retreated with a sensation of nervous shock in the solar plexus, then stricken with shame advanced more determinedly and found small holds at the outer edge of the chimney. The spray poured over my body, a constantly penetrating spur to hasten me upwards. At the very point where total immersion had seemed inevitable, I discovered some rock wrinkles that allowed me to push myself up, back and foot on opposing walls. My head, chest, and feet were thus clear of the main volume of water which instead poured onto my stomach. In one more minute I was standing on top, damp but delighted, and looking forward to the discomfiture of others. I was not disappointed. I have paid good money to see performing sea-lions give me a great deal less pleasure.

The first ascent of Clachaig Gully was followed by a 'first' ascent of Crowberry Gully on the Buachaille, with Murray completely unaware that, in fact, the route had already been climbed by Raeburn in 1909. But Bill Murray rated the Garrick Shelf of Crowberry Ridge as one of the best climbs he has done – a prototype of modern ice climbing.

Another route which followed the footsteps of Raeburn was Observatory Ridge on Ben Nevis in 1938 with Murray, MacKenzie and MacAlpine making the second ascent since Raeburn's original route eighteen years previously. They began the 900 foot (270 m) climb at half past nine in the morning and quickly discovered that it was not in good condition with two inches of wind-slab covering snow of quite sugary consistency. They took over four hours to climb the steep bottom section and encountered even worse snow conditions higher up on the most difficult pitches. The end of the route follows the top pitches of Zero Gully, and the party arrived there late in the day only to find loose snow covering hard, concrete-like, ice. By this time it was dark, so, using head torches, steps were cut all the way. When they reached the summit plateau it was almost mid-night, but a star studded sky welcomed them, and they took shelter for the night in the old observatory.

It seems that Murray had a penchant for finishing climbs in the dark. Indeed, he was a great devotee of moonlit climbing, an activity which he says with some sadness, is hardly ever done nowadays. He suggests that if you know the general layout of the route beforehand, climbing by torchlight is very nearly as good as climbing in daylight and in the right conditions you can get visibility of about forty miles. Head torches were certainly necessary on Murray's winter ascent of Tower Ridge on Ben Nevis. This has become a classic route, an ascent of the longest route on Britain's highest mountain, and in his graphic description of that climb in his book, *Mountaineering in Scotland*, Murray expertly weaves a spiritual dimension to the simple, physical act of climbing. It is an experience which comes to a climax as he walks across the Ben Nevis plateau after completing the route,

> Later, while we walked slowly across the plateau, it became very clear to me that only
> the true self, which transcends the personal, lays claim to immortality. On mountains,
> it is that spiritual part that we unconsciously develop. When we fail in that all other
> success is empty; for we take our pleasures without joy, and the ache of boredom
> warns of a rusting faculty.

Over fifty years after that climb, Bill Murray, now aged eighty, fondly remembers the details of the route with almost total recall,

> I was with Jimmy Bell and Douglas Laidlaw, a brilliant young climber who later joined
> the RAF and was killed in the war. We were led on, unsuspecting, by the appearance of
> the ridge which was heavily covered in snow. We had a late start, and climbed to the
> crest of the ridge by way of the Douglas Boulder, a big 700 foot buttress which sits at the
> foot of the ridge. This took some time because of the conditions, and by the time we
> reached the crest of the ridge it was beginning to become very windy indeed. The ridge
> is, I suppose, the better part of 2000 foot, and the way is barred by two towers. At first
> progress was easy, but it increased in difficulty as the ice and snow thickened as we
> gained height. When we reached the Great Tower, it was beginning to get dark. We

had to try and traverse round the east side of the Tower, rather than attack it direct. The rock became more and more icy, covered in *verglas* [thin rock-ice] and eventually, after a lot of very difficult ice climbing, we arrived in the Tower Gap, between the Great Tower and the final rocks which lead to the summit plateau. We were aware of two things, the wind, which was roaring through the gap sounding like an express train, and the sunset, which was absolutely fabulous. The sun was going down in a welter of cloud – there was a brilliant reddish sky and we were halted despite ourselves.

But when we tried to climb out of the Tower Gap the rock was so covered in thin ice that we couldn't get up. And the wind had become a hurricane – we had to hang on just to keep standing. After long delays and talk of retreat, one of the others suggested that I try and lasso a spire, like a canine tooth, which rose above the Gap. So, just as a last desperate measure, I tried it, and to our utmost surprise it went over a little bulge at the top and caught.

When we reached the summit plateau there was complete calm – the wind below was striking the cliffs and shooting vertically up into the air, leaving us in completely calm conditions. We all felt a profound relief and a deep sense of peace. It is always a very happy feeling getting to the top of any hard climb and one of the great things about mountains is that the memories are always good.

Those memories were to become very important to Murray in the years to come. Following his capture in the Western Desert (described at the beginning of this chapter) he was taken by the mountaineering tank commander to a prisoner-of-war camp on the Adriatic coast of Italy. It was there, desperately searching for a way to exercise his brain and take his mind off the horrors around him, that he started writing.

The trouble was that I had no paper, but fortunately, the Red Cross brought me a parcel from my mother which contained a lovely volume of the Works of William Shakespeare, printed on fine Indian art paper. It suddenly occurred to me that this would make a very fine toilet paper, and I could use the coarse Italian stuff for writing on. That's how it came about. I am sure the Bard would have approved.

When I started I could not remember enough incidents to fill one chapter, but with constant daily practice it all started coming back in technicolour. By practising the art of concentration I realized that the memory doesn't actually forget. All that one loses is the ability to pull material out of the pigeon holes through lack of

LAIDLAW, MURRAY AND BELL OUTSIDE THE CIC HUT ON BEN NEVIS, JUNE 1940.

practice and suddenly it was all coming back in abundance and I was able to write at reasonable speed. I kept these rolls of toilet paper inside my battle dress tunic, but later in 1943 the allied invasion of Italy began and we were moved first of all to a concentration camp in Bavaria, then to Marisch Tubia in Czechoslovakia. When we arrived there I was searched by the Gestapo who unfortunately found this mess of toilet paper hidden inside my tunic. They were convinced this was information I had been gathering about the German or Italian army and that I was going to pass it on to Czech patriots. I was interrogated at some length, but not beaten up as they fortunately observed the Geneva Convention. In the end they let me go, but I never saw the manuscript again.

ALASDAIR CAIN WITH THIRTIES' CLOTHING AND EQUIPMENT ON
THE EXPOSED EASTERN TRAVERSE OF TOWER RIDGE.

Most of us would have given up, the thought of starting all over again in such horrific circumstances being too much of a psychological barrier, but the tenacity which made Murray such a fine mountaineer turned what was a major setback, into a positive benefit.

In Czechoslovakia I did get good paper. This time I knew what I had to say so I was able to write faster and was actually able to improve greatly on the first version. I still kept the manuscript in my battle dress tunic because we had numerous searches, and it was a frightening time. Towards the end of the war we were all expecting the SS to

CLIMBERS GRAHAM MOSS, ALASDAIR CAIN AND MARK DIGGINS WHO 'BECAME'
MURRAY, BELL AND LAIDLAW FOR OUR RECONSTRUCTION OF
MURRAY'S ASCENT OF TOWER RIDGE.

come in and machine gun the lot of us – we had heard they were doing that in Eastern Europe, but we all found ways of taking our minds off that thought and for me it was living in the mountains in my imagination. Although we were on a starvation diet of 800 calories a day, rotten turnips and potato peelings one kept going mainly in the hope that the unexpected would happen and we would be released.

Murray returned to Britain and his book, which he called *Mountaineering in Scotland*, was accepted by the publishers, Dent. However, Dent wanted him to remove some of the passages which they thought were too spiritual but Murray refused, insisting that they were integral to the book, the circumstances of its writing and its subject matter. Today it is recognized as the classic account of climbing in Scotland between the two wars. It has inspired successive generations of Scottish climbers and has probably done more to popularize Scottish mountaineering than any other book, before or since.

By the end of 1950, Murray had widened his mountaineering experience by three visits to the Alps and a Himalayan expedition with Douglas Scott and Tom Weir. They enjoyed five months in the Garwhal area of India and Weir remembers that Murray spent a lot of time doctoring the sick who came to their camps. At this time thoughts were turning again to attempting the highest mountain on earth. British climbers had always been at the forefront of Himalayan exploration and there was a strong patriotic fervour to put a British climber on the summit of Everest. A real problem was that the north side of the mountain – the traditional pre-war approach through Tibet – was now closed, and the south approach was largely unexplored and thought to be unwise.

It seemed to Murray that the sensible thing to do would be to explore this Nepalese side of the mountain, so with a young army officer by the name of Mike Ward, he approached the Royal Geographical Society who, through its director Sir Lawrence Kirwan, agreed to give its blessing. He had discussions with the Alpine Club and it was decided that the Everest Committee, which had not met since before the war, should be re-convened. From the beginning, the Committee were reluctant to approach the mountain from the south and similar advice from the eminent explorer Bill Tilman seemed to confirm their belief, so it was only with great reluctance that they eventually agreed partially to sponsor the Murray/Ward expedition. Their sponsorship was not financial but they did agree to approach the Nepalese Government for permission to enter their country. To the consternation of the Everest Committee, the Nepalese willingly gave permission, so Murray, Ward and another climber, Tom Bourdillon, put £500 into a fund to help finance the expedition themselves. Unlike the Everest Committee, they appreciated the vital nature of the expedition for the Swiss were reported to be planning a large expedition to Everest in 1952 and the international race for the highest summit in the world was underway.

The following July the team was considerably strengthened by the inclusion of Eric Shipton, a highly respected explorer, and shortly afterwards, *The Times* offered a contribution of £5000 for the expedition dispatches. The final obstacle was overcome and they could now afford to go, but just as the expedition was about to set sail, a request arrived from the New Zealand Alpine Club asking if two of their members could join the trip. All but Shipton were against the idea but he won them round, suggesting that the two Kiwis could be got rid of if they were no use. One of the New Zealanders was Edmund Hillary.

WILLIAM HUTCHISON MURRAY SHOWING HIS MANUSCRIPT OF
MOUNTAINEERING IN SCOTLAND TO CAMERON MCNEISH.

The expedition was a great success and found a route up through the Western Cwm by which the mountain was eventually climbed. This was a vital reconnaissance for the 1953 expedition. Murray, as on his other Himalayan expedition, was affected by altitude sickness, and possibly because of that was not selected for the 1953 expedition. He was, however, in the Himalaya when Everest was climbed by Hillary and Tenzing. He discovered the news on buying a jar of honey wrapped in an Indian newspaper which he read. He was disappointed that the highest place on earth was no longer unclimbed.

Murray continued to climb in his beloved highlands, but did not try to compete with the new generation of climbers like John Cunningham, Tom Patey, Jimmy Marshall, Robin Smith and Hamish MacInnes. They were taking climbing into new realms of difficulty, and as Murray observed, '... had a speed and confidence we simply hadn't possessed. After we had climbed the Garrick Shelf on the Buachaille our immediate feeling was one of "never again". These fellows were starting with climbs like that, taking them almost for granted'. Another era was about to begin.

BUACHAILLE ETIVE MOR, KNOWN POPULARLY AS 'THE BUACHAILLE' (THE BIG
SHEPHERD) GUARDS THE ENTRANCE TO GLENCOE, AS IT RISES GRACEFULLY
FROM THE WIDE EXPANSE OF RANNOCH MOOR.

THE CREAGH DHU
AND OTHER STORIES...

In his book, *Always a Little Further*, first published in 1939, Alastair Borthwick reflected that eight years previously, 'fresh air was still the property of moneyed men, a luxury open to few'. Yet the thirties saw huge changes as the years of the depression encouraged many to leave the squalor of the cities. Mountaineer and broadcaster Tom Weir recalls that although Glasgow was a poor city in the thirties, it was still rich in green places. 'In those days' he remembers, 'there was plenty to explore on your own doorstep, and when motor cars were scarce, cycling was a pleasure'.

Many outdoor enthusiasts would congregate around the now legendary Craigallion fire, in a secluded pine-fringed hollow near Craigallion Loch, Milngavie. Here, most weekends, would be a fellowship of climbers and walkers, almost all working class lads swapping yarns and making plans. While the more affluent climbers of the day like W.H. Murray and his companions travelled north to Glencoe and Ben Nevis by motor car, this newer, working class group travelled less widely, and when they did go beyond their immediate vicinity, it was by foot or by hitchhiking. However, by the end of the thirties the growing popularity of hiking had an incredible effect. A chain of youth hostels grew across the highlands and lightweight tents became available. Many who did not like the rules of the youth hostel movement developed their own chain of simple accommodation – caves, howffs, and barns, generically known as dosses – and in some quarters, the hills were regarded as being unpleasantly overcrowded. Environmental problems were experienced too. The Craigallion fire was banned because of litter and Alastair Borthwick, amongst others, voiced the concern that 'cheapness and popularity have their dangers, particularly for those who climb. The sport is growing too quickly...'

Inevitably the dark shadow of the Second World War curtailed this new found activity. W.H. Murray, writing in *Mountain* in 1984 reflected,

> Then war swallowed us all up. We knew that in the last five years Scottish climbing had been re-founded, but dared not think of its future. As it happened, casualties in the second war, unlike the first, were low enough to ensure that this time no records were lost, standards were kept, and example given for a fast take-off by the young of the 'forties'.

Indeed, in some ways the Second World War had a positive effect. There was a new awareness of physical fitness by young men trained in survival skills and mountain warfare. There was better equipment including nylon ropes, stronger karabiners and vibram-soled boots, although the majority of climbers had to wait several years to see any of these.

Vibrams, named after their Italian inventor Vitale Bramani, were moulded rubber soles which began to replace the traditional nailed mountaineering boots from about 1947. But not everyone liked them. Controversy raged about their effectiveness. On wet grass and lichenous rock, or on hard snow and ice, they were potentially lethal, lacking the natural bite and grip of tricounis and nails. Conversely, they were lighter in weight, they were warmer, clung tenaciously to dry rock, and required less repair. And so they gradually replaced traditional boots, although the Aberdeen climbers sequestered (some would say deliberately) from the main opinion of Scottish mountaineering, continued to use nailed boots until well into the late fifties.

The other great breakthrough in equipment came with the advent of the nylon rope. In the past climbers caught in freezing winter weather would not be able to untie the hawser-like knots of their manila ropes, and would often have to wear their frozen rope until after reaching their car, hut or hotel. Nylon rope virtually ousted manila as soon as it became available in 1946-47. Its greater strength and elasticity offered additional safety, and its water-shedding properties gave a much welcomed suppleness.

After publishing *Mountaineering in Scotland* Murray began preparing the SMC's first rock climbing guide to Glencoe, encouraging a host of climbers in a new exploration of the Glencoe area. It was at this time that Scottish climbing began to experience the onslaught of the Creagh Dhu club. Here was the direct antithesis of the comparatively affluent middle-class SMC and JMCS. The Creagh Dhu was founded by Andy Sanders in 1930 in Clydebank, a working-class shipbuilding town, and the early members were all-rounders who used hill walking, climbing and travelling the byways as an escape from the depression. While the club was active in its early years, with Sanders teaming up with Jock Nimlin, the founder of the Ptarmigan Club, to climb a number of new routes including Nimlins Direct Route on the Cobbler, they made no real mark in Scottish mountaineering prior to the outbreak of war. After the war it was a different story. Localizing much of their activity in the Arrochar area, on the Cobbler and Beinn Narnain, and on Ben A'n in the Trossachs, the Creagh Dhu introduced artificial climbing, or continental tension-climbing, to Scotland. It was a technique commonly used on the big walls of the Italian Dolomites in the thirties and had become popular in the Alps.

The Creagh Dhu was characterized by their exciting and innovative style of climbing. It was the beginning of an era where rock climbing standards in Scotland mirrored those in England and Wales, and both rose dramatically. Indeed, the Creagh Dhu made the biggest impact on Scottish climbing since the golden days of the SMC at the turn of the century. They were soon followed by Aberdonian climbers under the inspiration of Bill Brooker and the redoubtable Tom Patey and later still, by Jimmy Marshall, Robin Smith and the 'Currie Boys' from near Edinburgh including Dougal Haston. Names like John Cunningham, Bill Smith, Charlie Vigano, Mick Noon, Pat Walsh, John McLean, George Shields and Hamish MacInnes were to virtually dominate climbing in the West of Scotland from the late forties until into the sixties. They put up a host of climbs which even today are regarded as hard, bold routes. They were the initial motivators behind a decade of climbing which was to see over 800 new routes climbed – 146 of them in winter – although the Creagh Dhu's contribution was primarily in summer rock climbing.

Yorkshireman Dennis Gray, for many years the General Secretary of the British Mountaineering Council spent a number of years living in Scotland, and regularly climbed with the Creagh Dhu. He recalls those days in his autobiographical work *Tight Rope*,

> This was a golden era for the Dhus and on my journey with them I grew to appreciate fully the initiative of working-class climbers in escaping from their awful inner-city environment, which appeared then to be a sea of slums and saloon bars, terribly depressing to a newcomer – but there was nothing depressed about my gregarious Glasgow friends, who joked and sang all the way to Arrochar. Every Dhu sported a flat cap, and they looked like the original No Mean City gang. Their accents were so

thick that I could barely follow their conversations, but it soon became apparent that, when the Dhus took a dislike to anyone it went deep, and in that era (like my own friends in the Bradford Lads) this dislike was directed towards the climbing establishment, which in Scotland then meant the SMC. However, they were not afraid of turning the joke on themselves, and I laughed until I cried at the misfortunes that had befallen them.

Edinburgh climber Jimmy Marshall first came across the Creagh Dhu in the Trossachs. Despite the myths that later suggested the Creagh Dhu were an introspective, aggressive bunch, Marshall's first recollection was how friendly they were. Friendly, but wild.

> They always climbed on Ben A'n because it was handy to get to from Glasgow. They took the bus over to Aberfoyle, then they'd hike over the Dukes Pass to the Trossachs and they had these tremendous thrashes there as well. They had a particularly famous one when they had this huge session in the bar, stole the targes and swords off the walls and they were running around in the snow, smashing the place up and thinking, 'this landlord's a bloody great guy, he's not doing anything about this'. The truth was that the police had become stuck in the snow on the way over.

The Creagh Dhu's Johnny Cunningham was, in 1951, an outstanding rock-climbing pioneer. This reputation was created by a host of first ascents, including Gallows Route and Guerdon Grooves on the Buachaille Etive Mor's Slime Wall, the latter a route far in advance of its time. Consider that Gallows Route, a strenuous and poorly protected line, was first climbed in 1947 in plimsolls – today it is graded at E1 5c. Edinburgh climber Kenny Spence, writing in *Mountain* in the mid-eighties, suggested that if 'modern' in rock-climbing means athletic and technical, as opposed to the romance of summits, and routes which finish on tops, then Cunningham's Gallows made him Scotland's first modern master. Guerdon Grooves, climbed with Bill Smith in 1948, is still a Hard VS and the original ascent was apparently watched by forty other members of the Creagh Dhu, some claiming it to be unjustifiable.

Cunningham served his time as a shipwright in John Brown's shipyard on Clydeside, a background shared by many of the Creagh Dhu. Like most of his contemporaries, Cunningham mainly climbed in summer in those early days, preferring to ski in winter. It was not until much later, when working with the British Survey in Antarctica that he began experimenting with front pointing techniques on ice and as

Hamish MacInnes demonstrating the 'Terrordactyl'
ice axe he designed.

Hamish MacInnes later recalled, 'he studied ballet at one time and used these skills to climb intimidatingly steep ice with razor keen crampons and an ice dagger'. Returning to the UK, Cunningham worked as an instructor at Glenmore Lodge and was one of the major technical innovators in the development of winter climbing, using two axes and the front points of crampons. Tragically, he was killed in 1979 while attempting to rescue a pupil from drowning off the cliffs of Anglesey in North Wales.

After the publication of Murray's SMC *Climber's Guide to Glencoe* in 1949, activity seemed to fall away for a few years but picked up again in 1954 with a series of impressive routes by Creagh Dhu members. Walsh and Vigano put up Brevity Crack (HVS) on the Buachaille, followed by Cunningham and Noon's Boomerang (VS) on Aonach Dhubh, with Walsh and Smith's Mainbrace Crack (HVS), and Walsh and Cunningham's Pendulum (E2), both of these again on the Buachaille. The following couple of years saw a blitz of other routes in Glencoe, with a number of new routes on Slime Wall by Patsy Walsh, including Bloody Crack (HVS), Revelation (VS) and Bludger's Route (HVS). But possibly the finest route of the time was Carnivore (E2) on Creagh a'Bhancair, by Cunningham and Mick Noon in 1958, with Dennis Gray later claiming that this route was the hardest he had ever climbed.

During the forties a young man from Greenock noticed that one of his neighbours rode off on his motor bike every Friday night, not returning till late on Sunday. Intrigued he asked the man where he went, and discovered he was a climber. The next weekend he went along as a pillion passenger. That chance encounter began a career which has been one of the most illustrious in Scottish mountaineering. Hamish MacInnes became a Creagh Dhu member and with an engineering background, was responsible for many of the technological advancements of the time, particularly in equipment but also in climbing techniques. In the early fifties he put up his share of new rock routes on the Cobbler, including Ithuriel's Wall (HVS), Gladiator's Groove Direct (HVS), Whither Wether (VS), and Whether Wall (VS). In 1953, a chance meeting with the young and inexperienced Chris Bonington led to first winter ascents of Agag's Groove (Grade V), on the Rannoch Wall of the Buachaille, and Raven's Gully (V), also on the Buachaille. Bonington later described MacInnes as 'already a legendary figure in Scottish circles, although he was only in his early twenties'. Born in Kirkudbrightshire, MacInnes had moved to Greenock with his family where his father had a shop. Later, he spent his National Service in Austria and had developed a panache for pegging routes; hammering pitons into cracks in the rock, clipping in a karabiner, and using the peg either as a running belay or for tension climbing. He soon developed a reputation for using pitons and earned the soubriquet of MacPiton. This habit did not endear him to the SMC and many of climbing's traditionalists, but Hamish was never one to allow public opinion to upset him too much. Later he moved to Glencoe where he founded the Glen's first official mountain rescue team.

In the north east, events were heralded by Bill Brooker's first climb of Giant's Head Chimney on Lochnagar. This was followed in December 1950 by the first winter ascent of the Douglas-Gibson Gully (Grade V) on Lochnagar by the emergent Tom Patey, and a whole host of new winter routes were to follow.

This Aberdeen School of climbers, as they came to be known, tended to apply themselves pretty strictly to winter buttresses, and mixed climbing, on granite, snow ice and frozen turf, became a major feature. Their exploratory climbing at this time opened up almost every major corrie in the Cairngorms and later, Creag Meagaidh. Throughout this post-war period there was tremendous competition between the various regional groups, or schools – the Creagh Dhu and SMC in the west, the Aberdeen school in the Cairngorms, and a growing band of hard climbers from the Edinburgh area, who were soon to dominate Scottish climbing in both the west and the east.

DOUGAL HASTON CLIMBING 'THE NOOK' ON THE COBBLER. THIS ROUTE IS
GRADED E2 AND THE FIRST ASCENT WAS MADE BY TWO CREAGH DHU MEMBERS, J.
CUNNINGHAM AND M. NOON IN 1955.

WHEECH, THE OLD MAN AND DOUGAL

ountaineering, in all its forms, has traditionally spawned a rich literature – one only has to consider the works of Mummery, Smythe, Stephen and Tilman to catch a glimpse of the rich vein of writing which has come out of the sport. In Scotland, W.H. Murray is still regarded as the doyen of mountain writers, but in the years following the post-war explosion in climbing standards in Scotland, four individuals stood head and shoulders above the rest, not only as immensely successful climbers, but also as naturally gifted in conveying the moods, resonances and experiences of their climbs to a growing audience of mountaineers. While there is no apparent reason why Scottish mountaineering should have produced four such talents at the same time, there is little doubt that the continuing popularity of the *Scottish Mountaineering Club Journal*, and a succession of enlightened editors, had a large part to play in it.

The four climbers who left such a legacy of literature pertaining to the late fifties and sixties are Tom Patey (see Chapter Seven) and three Edinburgh climbers who, although highly individualistic in character and personality, personify an era in which Scottish climbing breached a new dimension.

The Bat was the name given to what at the time, September 1959, was the hardest rock-climbing route in Britain (E2). Set on the Carn Dearg Buttress of Ben Nevis, it was a triumph for two young Edinburgh climbers, Robin Smith and Dougal Haston. The route was also a landmark for them as writers, with Smith's account, especially, capturing a memorable incident,

Now Dougal is a bit thick and very bold, he never stopped to think, he puts bits of left arm and leg in the crack and beat the rock ferociously...Then there came a sort of squawk... rattling sounds came from his throat or nails or something. It began under control as the bit of news 'I'm off', but it must have caught in the wind, for it grew like a wailing siren to a bloodcurdling scream as the black and bat-like shape came hurtling over the roof with legs splayed like webbed wings and hands hooked like a vampire.

Subsequently, Haston became one of Britain's best known mountaineers, a climber who was both charismatic and enigmatic and whose life was surrounded with controversy. By the time of his death in 1977, he had climbed throughout the world and his successes included an ascent of Everest, by the hitherto unclimbed South West Face, as one of the first British pair (with Doug Scott) to succeed on the World's highest mountain.

Robin Smith died some fifteen years earlier, aged only twenty three, while descending comparatively easy ground on Peak Garmo in the Russian Pamirs. Like Haston he was highly motivated; a mountaineer whose strength, competitiveness and perseverance were, according to one account, shattering.

Although quite different in character and temperament, Haston and Smith shared an interest in philosophy, and both developed into talented writers. At the time of his death Haston had completed his first novel, whilst Smith had published widely and was described by the editor of the SMC Journal as someone embarked 'on a search for a new form in mountaineering literature'.

The third member of that Edinburgh trio was Jimmy Marshall, who was once described by American climber, Yvon Chouinard, as being 'the real genius of the decade'. Six years older than Smith and eight years older than Haston, Marshall was the inspiration behind the climbing success of a wild bunch of lads from the Lothian village of Currie, of which Dougal Haston was a leading light and which included such luminaries as Jimmy Stenhouse and J. Moriarty, otherwise known as Big Elly.

But Marshall was also a brilliant climber in his own right. In a letter supporting his application to the SMC in 1955, Len Lovat suggested that in Marshall, the spirit of Raeburn has risen again. With a fierce determination, a powerful desire to explore new crags and tremendous natural ability, such a reincarnation was not beyond the bounds of possibility. According to Allen Fyffe, Marshall's great strength was his eye for a line particularly in winter.

ROBIN SMITH (LEFT) WITH FELLOW CLIMBER DAVEY AGNEW. THIS
PHOTOGRAPH WAS TAKEN SHORTLY BEFORE SMITH'S DEATH, AT
THE AGE OF TWENTY-THREE, IN PAMIRS.

He saw great routes, went out and climbed them, and each route was at the upper limit of what was being done at the time. Smith's Gully on Craig Meagaidh and Parallel Gully B on Lochnagar are just two that spring to mind. To me, if you go to any area and you pick up a guidebook and it says either Smith or Marshall as first ascensionists then you're pretty much guaranteed it is going to be a classic route that is really worth doing.

Writing in his collection of mountaineering essays, *On and Off the Rocks* in 1986, Jim Perrin suggested,

There is a little group of essays about climbs on Ben Nevis in the winter of 1959-60 which is quite unlike anything in climbing literature. Robin Smith's *The Old Man and the Mountains*, Jimmy Marshall's *Garde de Glace* and *The Orion Face*, and Dougal Haston's *Nightshift in Zero* have been quoted time and time again; certain passages from them appear to be the equivalent of the 'True Gospel' to any aspiring winter climber; they have given new words to the climbing vocabulary (I lose count of the number of times subsequent writers refer to their crampons scarting about in crumbly holds); they have the intrinsic gossipy interest of revealing what the respective authors thought of each other, and the routes described have inspired generations of climbers.

Today, Jimmy Marshall is a successful architect living in Edinburgh and claims his writings, and that of Smith, had the opposite effect to that which they originally desired. 'At the time we were sort of Messianic about Scottish winter climbing', he recalls, 'it was such a tremendous thing to us; dramatic, exciting – we were a bit nationalistic about it, like the Germans relationship with the Eiger, that was the romantic and daft way we thought about it. We wanted to write about it and try and get people winter climbing, but I think it had the reverse effect – it stopped them climbing, because they thought these things were too difficult'.

Perhaps that was not surprising, since Marshall, according to Perrin, had a refreshingly direct and descriptive style, as in this passage from his essay *The Orion Face*,

> Following up was like walking on eggs, the dark pit beneath our heels sufficient
> warning to take care; a short step of ice above Wheech [Robin Smith] led on to the
> high snow slopes which form beneath the terminal towers of the Orion Face. Here
> the expected respite failed to materialise; knee deep and floury, they whispered evil
> thoughts, threatening to slide us into the black void and extinguish the winking
> lights of the CIC Hut.

Marshall's mountaineering roots are very similar to that of many of his contemporaries, wandering the local hills, the Pentlands, as a schoolboy. The first climbers he met were rock climbers in Skye – 'and bloody awful specimens they were too!'

Later Marshall made up a lasting friendship with a climber called Bill Cole, and finding some rock climbing notes written by Jock Nimlin, a discovery which must have been like gold in those days, they were off to Ben A'n in the Trossachs. This was about 1949, and even at that time, Marshall was well aware of the Creagh Dhu club's reputation as the principal movers of rock climbing development in Scotland,

> Cole's sister was courting a lad from Glasgow, and he kept referring to the Creagh Dhu,
> in hushed, reverential tones... we were well aware of what they were doing and the
> standards they were setting.

Their first meeting was on Ben A'n, and Marshall recalls finding members of the infamous club sitting around on the summit rock proudly watching their star, Johnny Cunningham, demonstrate his prowess.

He was on a direct finish to a route called The Last 80, one of the classic routes at Ben A'n. There's a pull up at the end onto a spar that sticks out, and Johnny was climbing in his customary jeans and flat cap. All the other guys were just sitting around watching him. Bill and I were thinking that it looked bloody easy, and these Creagh Dhu guys were having a go after Cunningham and falling off, and trying it again and falling off again. Only Cunningham and another Creagh Dhu, George Shields, could do it and they climbed it so smoothly that it looked easy. As soon as they moved away we were up there having a go, and we just couldn't make anything of it. We thought we were good because we had done everything else on Ben A'n, so it brought us back to earth with a bump.

Shortly after that Marshall got to know many of the Creagh Dhu lads and found them, contrary to the myths and legends, to be a very friendly bunch,

> They could be extremely wild, but I always got on very well with them. They were also very helpful and would give you a lot of information. This Glasgow versus Edinburgh thing is a bit of myth.

Despite the Creagh Dhu's affability towards Marshall, there certainly was rivalry in Scotland at the time, particularly between the various regional factions. It increased in passion a few years later in 1958 when Marshall and Graham Tiso had the audacity to breach the Aberdonian Ice Curtain and bag the first ascent of Parallel Gully B on Lochnagar.

> That really came from the information in the journals. I read a tremendous article by Patey about the ascent of Parallel B in summer. There was a photograph of it and I was convinced it looked like a perfect winter route. I immediately thought what a wonderful spoof it would be to irritate the Aberdeen lads. That was really what was behind it – that was the icing on the cake.

Allen Fyffe, at that time studying geography at Aberdeen University and very much part of the Aberdeen school, remembers that first ascent, and how it infuriated the Aberdeen climbers,

That ascent of Parallel B was always a sore point with the Aberdonians. It was a really

sore point, in fact. Jim MacArtney and myself managed to do the second ascent of the
route and we did it in a better time. In those days all the guide books gave times for
winter routes and Parallel B was something like eight hours and we managed to do it
in under six, so we felt that a bit of the aura had been reclaimed, but Marshall was the
man who got it first.

Jimmy Marshall claimed many first ascents during a career which saw him excel in both
winter and summer. When asked what he considers to be his best rock climbing route
he answers tongue in cheek, 'like my bairns, I love them all', but when pressed plumps
for Trapeze, a 455 foot (138 m) route on the east buttress of Aonach Dubh in Glencoe
which today is graded at E1.

> That was a lovely climb. Len Lovat and myself were coming down the glen from Stob
> Coire nam Beith, and Lovat pointed out a wonderful corner high up on the buttress
> above us. A couple of years later, in 1960, somebody told Smith about it and I arrived
> back from the Alps to discover that he had been up trying it the day before. I
> thought… I had better get moving. So, Doug Leaver and I went up and just cruised it
> really. The funny thing was, I never used much protection, I would have used it if I
> could have got it in but I could not, so I just had to go for it. I remember hooking my
> arm over this chockstone and it moved down about a foot, then we went round this
> corner, and we hadn't even looked at it from below to work out where the route
> would go. We just knew we were going to climb the corner, and what we found was a
> very steep leaning wall with big flat topped holds. I went round first and found this
> long groove going up, so I just followed that.
>
> The route's called Trapeze because Leaver came off trying to come up this steep
> overhanging wall and instead of falling downwards, he just swung round in this
> magnificent arch – I couldn't actually see him as he was climbing, but I just saw this
> wonderful sight of him going Wheee… away across this tremendous drop above No 4
> Gully and swinging in again. That was very impressive…

Despite his successes and a whole string of innovative, hard first ascents, in both summer
and winter, Jimmy Marshall is very quick to play down his role as one of the main devel-
opers of Scottish mountaineering in the fifties and sixties. He forcibly, even aggressively,
makes the point that climbing was developed throughout that era by a wide array of

climbers, from the Creagh Dhu in the west, Aberdeen climbers in the Cairngorms, and a bunch of Edinburgh climbers which included Smith, Haston and himself. But Marshall is keen to reinforce the point he made in Smith's obituary in the SMC Journal, that Robin Smith was undoubtedly the greatest climber of that generation to join the club, and possibly the most outstanding mountaineer throughout the long and varied history of the Scottish Mountaineering Club. It is an incredible accolade for one so young.

Marshall first met Robin Smith in 1953 when Smith was in his final couple of years at school.

> He was very independent even then, and he didn't like to lean on any of us – he loved the company and he loved the chat but he was very much his own independent self – with a very powerful personality.

Despite that independence and personality, Smith started climbing as a fairly quiet, inordinately shy boy and ignoring the advice of older, more experienced climbers, immediately started climbing some of the harder routes of the day, spurred on by a bubbling enthusiasm. So, did Marshall immediately realize the great natural talent which was being exhibited?

> No, but we noticed him which was surprising. We wouldn't normally have noticed anyone, and it is hard to separate that with what took place later, but he was noticeable by his competitive edge.

It was partly that hard competitive edge, coupled with a raw anarchism towards authority, that antagonized many people. Dressed in his short Italian jacket, drain-pipe trouser legs tapered into pointed suede shoes, many regarded him as too streetwise. Marshall watched Smith mature into the hardest climber of them all, with a strength and perseverance that was shattering.

> Robin had this amazing ability, but whilst he could easily cruise an existing route, he seemed incapable of cruising his new routes like we did. Our style was more fluent, but he could stick like a limpet to the rock. He was small with bandy legs, a bit like Whillans although he was more thick-set than Whillans was when he was young. It was the same in winter, he could stick on the stuff. On our winter ascent of Smith's Route on Gardyloo Buttress, he cut for six hours to overcome the near vertical 150 foot prow of the ice-plated buttress.

Jimmy Marshall, six years older than Smith, was always referred to as The Old Man. Smith, in return, in later writings, was always called Wheech, an unusual nickname, the origins of which suggest something of Smith's character at the time.

> Robin liked to discomfit people! Particularly on climbs. He'd be somewhere up a crag with some poor chap – because he'd climb with absolutely anybody, and as the second was getting into these horrendous difficulties all you'd hear from up above was this 'wheech, wheech, wheech, wheech', as he laughed away in this wee high pitched laugh that he had. It was the Currie boys who gave him the name, probably because they heard it so often.

By December 1958, when he applied to join the SMC, Smith's application form contained a formidable list of first ascents. In the early summer of the following year, spurred on by a nationalistic pride which recognized a possible new line between two routes put up by Englishmen, Brown and Whillans' Sassenach (HVS) and Centurion (HVS), Smith and Dick Holt attempted this unclimbed central corner on the Carn Dearg Buttress of Ben Nevis. After a late start, very much the norm for Smith, darkness overtook them before they reached the corner proper, and they climbed the top section of Sassenach instead. Smith returned in the autumn, this time with Dougal Haston, and a shambolic pair they appeared to be. Smith later wrote in his famous essay *The Bat and the Wicked*,

> I was the only climber Dougal could find, and the only climber I could find was Dougal, so we swallowed a very mutual aversion to gain the greater end of a sort of start over the rest of the field.

Haston had a decent pair of rock climbing shoes, PAs as they were called, while Smith's kletterschuhs had seen better days. In effect they started the route with one pair of decent shoes between them and had to swop over between pitches. Their ropes were little better. Haston's had lost five feet of its length due to an experiment on the Currie railway wall, while Smith's, which was apparently on loan, had been stretched a bit, so it was now ten feet longer than its original 120 feet (36 m). Climbing on two ropes, Smith solved the problem of different rope lengths by wrapping the longer one 'round and round my middle to make the two ropes even'.

ROBIN SMITH CAMPING IN GLENCOE WHERE HE PUT UP A
NUMBER OF FINE ROUTES INCLUDING SHIBBOLETH AND YO-YO.

The climb turned out to be an epic, with the pair swapping leads and the difficulties. All went fairly well until Haston thought he could make out a ledge above an overhanging roof and set out to reach it, but, 'in my over-confidence I'd hopelessly underestimated the angle of the corner. Overhanging it was, and my ledge didn't exist. I found myself with fingers stuck despairingly into a turf that was sliding'.

This was when Haston took his now famous bat-like fall, a fall which also succeeded in pulling Smith from his stance so that both climbers were suspended from a wooden wedge hammered into a crack in case of such an eventuality. They both scrambled back on to the rock and in the growing nightfall, called it a day. The next week the pair returned, and this time Smith had a decent pair of rock climbing boots. They quickly achieved their previous high point and this time Smith had a go at the overhanging roof. Twice he fell off, but with little intention of allowing Haston an opportunity to lead he suggested he would just retrieve some protection gear.

77

JIMMY MARSHALL ON CROWBERRY RIDGE, BUACHAILLE ETIVE MOR,
WHERE THE ROUTE ENGINEER'S CRACK JOINS UP WITH FRACTURE ROUTE.

So I was very sly and said we had to get the gear and climbed past the roof to the sling
at the pebbles leaving all the gear in place. There I was so exhausted that I put in a
piton, only it was very low, and I thought, so am I, *peccavi, peccabo*, and I put in
another and rose indiscriminately until to my surprise I was past Dougal's ledge and
still on the rock...

This was the key to the climb and Smith had solved it. Haston followed, then led, the
next pitch. The Scots had proved their point, and as Ken Crocket later suggested
'probably helped salve the wounds inflicted by Centurion and Sassenach'.

The following winter, Smith and Marshall returned to the Ben to enjoy what was
meant to be a swan-song for Marshall. Towards the end of 1959 Marshall had become
disenchanted with climbing because of a long run of wet weekends and had decided to
concentrate his future efforts into building up his architects business. This was to be a
final fling before he got married. It didn't quite work out like that.

I had become so pissed off with the weather that summer. It rained, rained, rained, so
I thought, to hell with this. I had no intention of packing climbing in completely, but
I had enough of this crap of going off every weekend into the rain.

Ken Crocket suggests that in this week Smith and Marshall 'were to bring to a climax
the end of a decade of exciting developments in Scottish mountaineering. In one sense,
they were to gain a pinnacle of achievement which can never be bettered'.

He has since described the week as 'pivotal', a week that saw the two mountaineers
climb the first ascent of Great Chimney on Tower Ridge, giving it a Grade IV, the first
ascent of Minus Three Gully (Grade IV), the first ascent of Gardyloo Buttress via
Smith's Route (Grade V a route which had to wait eleven years for a second ascent),
the first winter ascent of Observatory Buttress (Grade V), the second ascent of the
notorious Point Five Gully (Grade V), the first winter ascent of Pigott's Route on the
Comb (Grade IV), and finally, the first long awaited ascent of Orion Face (Grade V);
a route up a great face demanding a wide range of climbing skills; which seemed to
augur the shape of things to come. It was later described by Marshall as a 'super week's
climbing', but Ken Crocket believes it be of much greater significance.

> The first winter ascent of the Orion Face was the climax of an incredible week of
> mountaineering on Ben Nevis. The partnership of Smith and Marshall had joined
> with ideal conditions. But it was more than that. In the ten years that followed other
> fine and equally hard routes would be won by step cutting. But no other climber
> would come near to repeating such a sustained effort, nor to writing about their climbs
> with such sustained feeling. Just as Murray had been a source of inspiration to them, so
> their gripping essays, Marshall's *The Orion Face* and Smith's *The Old Man* and *Mountains*
> represent vivid accounts of climbing of the time.

Jimmy Marshall looks back to that week with great fondness, but does not give it special
significance.

> Really that was just an accident that we got together and climbed then. I've objected
> to its undue prominence, because people were doing magnificent climbs – I think of
> the Sticil Face in the Cairngorms climbed by Grassick – all of these routes were

79

simply things that we wanted to do. We were also lucky to get a week like that, because we were at the peak of our form.

Neither was Marshall aware at the time of the significance that week would be given:

> We were only pleased at having done the Orion. Smith knew about it and had heard about it from the Currie boys who had let the information slip, so he thought that would be a great thing to do. But the idea that it would be the ultimate of fine lines to climb in winter was silly. It was certainly different from things that had gone previously, although it now transpires that its not really very different from all the other things that were going on elsewhere.

At this time, early 1960, the other member of that Edinburgh trio, Dougal Haston, had just entered Edinburgh University where he studied philosophy. In the year up till then he had been climbing more or less full-time, living on the dole and shuttling backwards and forwards between Edinburgh and Glencoe to collect his weekly unemployment benefit. He was not popular with the climbing establishment of the time, and had created a running feud with the SMC. This came to a head when he took it on himself to re-decorate the interior of the SMC's Lagangarbh Hut below the Buachaille. Haston took some red and yellow paint and splashed a weird assortment of shapes and symbols around the walls, which in fact had just been recently painted by an SMC work-party. Marshall knew Haston in all his moods and made this assessment of his character,

> There's been a lot of rubbish talked about Dougal, about his so-called black side. I remember describing him to one of the SMC lads as an evil black bastard! That's how I assessed Dougal, because we had never met people like that in these days. They came afterwards, in the punk era, but he was probably ten years ahead of the punk revolution. And although he was probably the lead figure in terms of this wildness, the other boys aided and abetted him and expressed it even more violently.
>
> As an example, Dougal wasn't particularly aggressive, but if you went out to the pubs on a Saturday, you always met the Saturday night punchers, the lads looking for fights. They always wanted to fight Big Elly, because he stood head and shoulders above everybody else, and they would work towards our group and usually they knocked my brother Ronnie, or spilt his beer, and blamed him for starting a fight. Yet

DOUGAL HASTON ON GARROTTE, NORTH BUTTRESS,
BUACHAILLE ETIVE MOR.

Dougal used to go out with a karabiner round his fist, and when we went outside for the battles Big Elly, who was a beautiful boxer, used to clock people and thump them over, but Dougal would fight with this karabiner as a knuckleduster. That says a lot.

But he did mature, into a tremendous individual. He's a very dear friend of mine, and always was. I know his family well too. He wasn't as good a climber as Robin but he had tremendous grit. He would have a go at anything, even if he was unable to do it he would push the boat right out.

Like Marshall and Smith, Dougal Haston also developed into a fine writer and his essay *Nightshift in Zero*, published in the *Edinburgh University Mountaineering Club Journal*

DOUGAL HASTON AFTER CONTROVERSIALLY 'REPAINTING' THE
SCOTTISH MOUNTAINEERING CLUB'S LAGANGARBH HUT, GLENCOE.

in 1960 is a good example of the promise to come, a promise which culminated in his biography, In *High Places*, published in 1972. In this extract Haston described the approach of night on Zero Gully,

> We had a ten-minute session and then I got the urge to lead and started up the next pitch. This got me gripped and eventually I stopped under an ice-bulge leaving a line of buckets to salute the evening sun which was charging down with so much haste that it forgot to tell the moon to come up so that it was getting dark rather quickly. Andy was brought up to Wheech and Wheech was brought up to me and proceeded on to the bulge. This was mountaineering at its wonderful best; the still lonely silence of glorious nature in all its twilit splendour was broken only by the sweet schoolboyish voice of Wightman uttering foul vicious oaths and tirades against the certainty of the origins of his partners on the rope.

Perhaps his most enduring route in Scotland, other than The Bat, was Hee Haw (E1) on the west face of Aonach Dubh in Glencoe, climbed with Moriarty in 1959. Haston was to disappear from the Scottish scene for a time following a road accident in Glencoe in which a hill walker was knocked down and killed. It was later, in the Alps and in the Greater Ranges, that Dougal Haston was to become virtually a household name as the hero of the first winter ascent of the infamous Eiger Nordwand, the first ascent of the South Face of Annapurna and, along with Doug Scott, the first British ascent of Mount Everest by the previously unclimbed South West Face.

In the late sixties he went to live in Switzerland as the Director of the International School of Mountaineering at Leysin, and it was there in January 1977 that he was killed in an avalanche while skiing a steep *couloir* near his home. Chris Bonington, the team leader on both the successful Annapurna and Everest expeditions, described Haston as one of the most charismatic British climbers of the postwar era. In his book *The Everest Years* Bonington suggests that Dougal Haston was very difficult to get to know, putting forward that very few people really managed to get close to him. He also recalls that at the end of the International Everest Expedition of 1971, in which nationalistic prejudices and constant personal bickering were the hallmarks, Haston was one of the few members of the team who had made no enemies. Jimmy Marshall, who was probably closer to Haston than any other climber, endorses this view that Haston 'did mature, into a tremendous individual, one of my dearest friends'.

The fifties and sixties saw a huge explosion in interest in climbing and mountaineering in Scotland, with standards rising proportionally. While the Creagh Dubh in the west of Scotland, and Marshall *et al* in the East were leading the way, another school of climbing was establishing itself in the far north east of Scotland, a group of characters who were happy to explore their own lairs of Lochnagar and the Cairngorms, making only occasional sorties into the hills of the west. Out of this stronghold was born one of the most charismatic Scottish mountaineers of the century.

THE OLD MAN OF STOER OFF THE SUTHERLAND COAST NEAR LOCHINVER. IT WAS
FIRST CLIMBED BY PATEY, ROBERTSON, HENDERSON AND NUNN IN 1966.

CHAPTER SEVEN:

DOCTOR TOM

Scottish mountaineering has produced a plethora of strong characters over the last century but few have matched the lasting charisma of Tom Patey. When he died in an abseiling accident after climbing The Maidens, a quartzite sea-stack off Whiten Head, Sutherland on 25 May 1970, it brought to an end a tremendous mountaineering career which lasted twenty years. To the public at large he was known only through the Old Man of Hoy BBC television spectacular in 1967, but inside the small climbing world he was a renowned figure. He was loved and respected by his peers. From his very first ascent on Lochnagar's Douglas-Gibson Gully in 1950 to his last climb, which led to his premature death at the age of 38, he was a major player on the Scottish climbing scene.

But Patey was more than just an exceptional climber – he was an exceptional character: a singer, story-teller, pianist and accordionist, he was always the life and soul of any party. He was also the uncrowned king of climbing satire and his posthumously published book, *One Man's Mountains*, gives an insight into his unique humour, which is interwoven through the essays and songs superbly catching the spirit of Scottish climbing during the fifties and sixties.

It was a visit to Bob Scott's bothy at Luibeg, a stones throw from Derry Lodge on the Braemar side of the Cairngorms, that was to fire the ambition of the future mountaineer. This bothy was a haven for climbers. Friday nights in winter would see a succession of rucksack-burdened Aberdonians trudge the seemingly interminable miles from the car park at Linn of Dee, longing to see the faint but cheering glow of the lights from the stalker's kitchen window. Often, as you approached the rickety shelter which adjoined the house, you would hear song and laughter, the camaraderie of climbers, encouraged and led on by Bob Scott himself. Bob, despite the isolated position of his keeper's house near the junction of Glen Luibeg and Glen Derry, was a gregarious sort, and looked forward to the weekend visits of these unkempt mountaineers.

One of those mountaineers was Bill Brooker, now a retired lecturer and a long time member of the Scottish Mountaineering Club. He recalls the Hogmanay of 1949 and describes it as 'a memorable occasion'. The weather was incredibly cold, perhaps twenty below, so cold that the hole in the ice for the water bucket had to be re-opened every day. But inside the bothy the deep hay offered a warm and comfortable bed – if you could find a spot to lie down.

The bothy was bulging with climbers on holiday. Over forty of them were housed in various outbuildings, with the main bothy, and its roaring log fire, reserved for the hierarchy. It was into this happy melée that a small group of youths appeared, and were instantly consigned to the stick shed. The lads were happy enough with the arrangement, despite the fact that snowdrifts had formed inside the walls and an indoor thermometer recorded −40 degrees Centigrade. But even the stick shed would be a luxury compared to the previous night which they had spent on the summit of Ben MacDhui in atrocious conditions. Some of them wore the kilt and Bob, who was always keen to take the mickey, especially at self-inflicted misfortune, labelled the little band the 'Horrible Hielanders'. One of those Horrible Hielanders was Tom Patey. Later that year he was to enter Aberdeen University to study medicine, yet he continued in the same group, ill-clad and ill-equipped, but climbing Munros in all weathers.

Thomas Walton Patey was born in Ellon, just north of Aberdeen, in 1932. A son of the Episcopalian minister, he became a Boy Scout and discovered the hills. Weekends and holidays were spent roaming the nearby Cairngorms, but there was something missing from these innocent wanderings which Patey later identified in a wonderful essay, *Cairngorm Commentary*, published in the *SMC Journal* of 1962.

> Adventure, unconventionality, exuberance – these were the very elements missing from our scholarly conception of mountaineering which had led us with mechanical precision up and down the weary lists of Munros Tables.

Patey described his little group as mere 'hill bashers', compared to the 'real' mountaineers like Bill Brooker and his climbing companion of the time, Mac Smith,

> Mac Smith was then the chieftain of the Luibeg Clan, an all-round mountaineer who had taken part in almost every important summer or winter ascent in recent years. He knew the Cairngorms better than any of his contemporaries, and they would have been the first to admit it. The bothy armchair, which has only recently been vacated

TOM PATEY, ONE OF BRITAIN'S MOST PROLIFIC CLIMBERS
IN BOTH SUMMER AND WINTER.

and converted into firewood, was Mac's prerogative – a rustic throne. Bill Brooker,
'the young Lochinvar', cut a more dashing figure, the complete counterpart to Mac's
slightly reserved manner. To all outward appearances he was merely another pimply-
faced schoolboy like ourselves, full of wild talk. But then who could forget that this
was the same young heretic who had but recently burst into the climbing arena with a
series of routes which had defied the best efforts of preceding generations? With such
a wealth of mountaineering experience behind him, you could overlook the lads
extravaganzas.

But it was not long before those attributes of adventure, unconventionality and exuberance became a very real part of young Patey's lifestyle. Eager to be identified with what he regarded as 'the select conclave that gathered in the Fife Arms, Braemar, on a Saturday night', he began to explore the crags of the Buchan sea-cliffs north of Aberdeen, and some of the well-trodden scrambles of Lochnagar and the Cairngorms.

Patey's skill expanded with his growing experience, and so did his attitude. As he gradually discovered a natural aptitude for climbing he became aware of another great talent – a skill that not every climber is graced with. He had a tremendous sense of judgement on how safe a move was likely to be and this allowed him to stretch himself and climb closer to his own limits than some other climbers.

One of the reasons was that Patey did not like to use ropes – he believed in the old dictum that the leader must not fall, therefore what was the point in him being encumbered with a rope? He believed that a solo climber was a safe climber, basing his simple logic on the fact that if he were anything other than safe, he would be dead. His attraction in solo climbing was the freedom of movement he enjoyed, a sensation similar to 'coasting down the motorway after being held up at every set of traffic lights in Glasgow. You keep in top gear and your performance improves correspondingly'.

While some climbing partners were unnerved by Patey's apparent nonchalance, others shared it, including Hamish MacInnes. He enjoyed climbing with Tom Patey more than anyone else. 'Much of our climbing was done solo together as he used to call it. Some of his enthusiasm for this fast technique rubbed off on me, and one certainly had a fine sense of freedom climbing this way'. But some of Patey's erstwhile companions recall his other climbing idiosyncrasies. He was not the most graceful of mountaineers. Bill Brooker remembers the alarming grunts and heaves which accompanied Patey's earlier climbing, and Tom Weir recalls a similar style when he climbed with Patey on Eagle Ridge of Lochnagar,

> As an introduction to rock-climbing on Lochnagar it was a real test of adhesion for
> me on holdless, slippery granite, hands half frozen in the falling sleet. But Tom was
> exuberant as he scraped, lunged, grunted, drawing breath only to extol some feature
> of the elegant route that I might be missing.

Bill Brooker, who became a regular climbing partner, can recall him falling only once, during a winter ascent of Mitre Ridge Direct on Beinn a'Bhuird in 1953, whilst Dennis

Gray admits he had never seen anyone climb quite like him. He felt Patey was ungainly, 'but' says Gray, 'he was truly effective in simply getting up climbs with speed, and, on mixed ground or easy grade rock or ice, he was a whirlwind of movement'.

It was another route on Lochnagar that gained Patey's admittance to that select band of Aberdeen climbing's hierarchy. In December 1950, with Goggs Leslie, he made the first winter ascent of Douglas-Gibson Gully, the most fearsome of Lochnagar's gullies. Harold Raeburn had looked closely at this route in 1901, and had been lowered down on a rope, only to suggest that he was 'sufficiently discouraged by what he saw not to try again'.

The gully was eventually climbed in 1933 by Charles Ludwig in summer conditions, but despite several attempts by Aberdonian climbers, the winter ascent remained inviolate. Patey and Leslie's ascent signified a new era in Scottish winter climbing. Bill Murray described it as a '*tour de force* without parallel in Scotland', a snow and ice ascent of what had previously been considered to be purely a rock route. More impressively Tom Patey was only eighteen.

While Patey believed that the route earned him a 'grudging acceptance' from his more talented contemporaries, Ken Grassick was more benevolent in his praise. Describing the route as 'amazing', he recalls the night, two years later, that Patey appeared at the door of Lochend Bothy near Lochnagar. This howff was regarded as the domain of the Boor Boys, or the Corrour Club, 'a motley collection of ex-grammar schoolboys, "brigands of the bothy", who enforced a regular reign of terror on a community where misanthropes and ornithologists were rife'.

> In spite of our usual unpleasantness to strangers, we were quietly pleased that such a great climber should want to befriend us and welcomed him. Next day he chose me as his climbing companion and on Eagle Ridge and Black Spout Pinnacle I climbed far beyond my previous levels. That day was the only day I ever kept up with Tom on the approaches. He usually forged ahead of his party to be waiting, calm and rested, at the top of the first pitch as we arrived at the foot in a breathless and laboured rush. I later discovered that this was a favourite tactic employed to maintain or confirm his top-dog position in the pack, especially if competition threatened.

Throughout the years, several of Patey's regular climbing companions have admitted he had faults, but as Grassick himself suggests, 'they passed affectionately as eccentricities'.

He carried very little food with him. Nor was he a great believer in carting great loads of equipment. Ken Grassick painted a vivid picture of the dishevelled, Patey, striding towards the climb seemingly oblivious to the discomforts of the untidy rope, which trailed behind him. Another contemporary suggests that Patey showed a great lack of concern about his clothes, possessions and even climbing equipment. He often did his hard winter climbs clad inadequately in borrowed and ill-fitting equipment.

Even in later years as a doctor (and he was always considered to be an outstanding medic) he had his eccentricities. On the Mustagh Tower expedition in 1956, Joe Brown, at that time Britain's finest rock climber, was disconcerted to find Patey's

> medical gear in complete disarray. I remember him picking a syringe up out of the sand and it was full of it so that when he squeezed it, it broke. I thought… what a way to handle medical kit!

Dennis Gray describes Patey as

> the most unlikely looking doctor I have yet come across, for he looked more like a boxer than a Dr Finlay. Powerfully built, of medium height and with bushy dark hair, he had a face which looked as if it had been hewn from the granite of his native country.

In those early years of the fifties, exploration of the Cairngorms was entering a particularly active phase and whilst Patey's Douglas Gully opened the floodgates, better, more technical routes followed. Patey himself, accompanied by Ken Grassick and Graeme Nicol climbed the 690 foot (210 m) Scorpion on Carn Etchachan; Eagle Ridge was climbed by Patey, Mike Taylor and Bill Brooker; Brooker and Patey climbed Mitre Ridge on Beinn a'Bhuird; Ken Grassick climbed Polyphemus Gully; Grassick and Nicol put up the superb Sticil Face of Shelter Stone Crag above Loch Avon. Meanwhile, Patey was making some raids into the west, putting up his Central Pillar of Coire Ardair on Creag Meagaidh, a route generally regarded as a modern classic. Yet despite the rivalries between the climbers of east and west, Tom Patey was never secretive or selfish about new routes or new crags.

His infectious enthusiasm was above such petty rivalries and Bill Brooker believes it was this which fostered the growth of the Aberdeen School of the later 1950s. This group embraced mountaineering as opposed to pure rock climbing, and mixed winter climbing rather than pure ice climbing. A good example of Patey's disregard for regional rivalries was demonstrated during the winter of 1957 on Ben Nevis. On either side of Observatory Ridge, the Nevis cliffs are riven by two deep gullies, Zero Gully and Point Five Gully, both vertical and bulging with overhanging ice. Both had been attempted several times by an assortment of strong climbing parties. Patey and Graeme Nicol arrived at the CIC Hut on Ben Nevis, to be joined the next day by a group of climbers from Glasgow. Unfortunately a strong south-west wind was blowing waves of snow and spindrift down the main gullies, so Patey and Nicol took themselves off to try the Cresta Climb, while the Glaswegians attempted North East Buttress. On their return to the hut, Patey and Nicol were rather put out to realize that the party in the CIC Hut had been enlarged by two more climbers; 'whose characteristic patois, coupled with a distinct air of authority, stamped them as members of the Creagh Dhu'.

John Cunningham and Mick Noon were two of the Creagh Dhu club's boldest climbers, and they immediately announced their plans to climb Zero Gully the next day, 'without apparently noticing the disquieting effect this had on the rest of the company'. As the climbers settled themselves in for the night the door of the hut suddenly burst open to reveal a dishevelled figure, 'and the self-appointed guardian of Zero Gully stood before us'. Hamish MacInnes had a somewhat proprietorial attitude regarding Zero Gully. Instructing on a course at Steall Hut in Glen Nevis, he heard news that the vultures were gathering below his route and set off across the Carn Mor Dearg Arete, intent on making his presence felt. Cunningham and Noon were disconcerted by the arrival of MacInnes, but resignedly agreed to climb with him. It was settled – the Creagh Dhu would be going for Zero Gully. The climbers were virtually avalanched off the route, and Cunningham and Noon returned to Glasgow that night, after chastizing MacInnes who had indicated he would team up with the Aberdonians for another attempt. Like Patey, MacInnes was uninterested in petty regional or club rivalries.

It was in superb condition with plenty of snow-ice, and MacInnes and Patey shared the lead through the initial vertical corner, with Patey using single-rope tension from ice-pitons, and MacInnes front pointing between pitons. Within five hours they reached the plateau. Ironically, after a previous attempt MacInnes had written in the CIC Hut log book, 'this climb is not possible in one day'. On topping out into the sunshine of the plateau MacInnes declared it a great climb: 'Up to Raven's Gully standard!' Nicol, not to be undone, retaliated with North East fervour, 'It might even hold its own on Lochnagar!' Patey later recalled that they were still arguing as they reached the hut.

In the late fifties and early sixties, many young people in Scotland were caught up in the great revival of traditional folk music that was sweeping through Britain. This social scene was immensely attractive to Tom Patey. When he was eventually elected to that select band which met in the Fife Arms Hotel on Saturday nights it was soon discovered that he played the piano and harmonica – in fact he promoted the kazoo bands which became such a prominent feature of such weekends. But it was the accordion which became his first love, and once he discovered its versatility, he was rarely parted from it.

Patey was a born entertainer and, without peer, climbing's musical minstrel. His satirical songs, like 'Onward Christian Bonington', 'MacInnes's Mountain Patrol', (dedicated to 'Scotland's leading philanthropist and his gallant pack of Avalanche Dogs') and the 'Ballad of Bill Murray', have become classics of mountain literature. But, as Jim Perrin has pointed out, there is little savagery in his satire, and he never attempted anything like character assassination.

> Something kindlier than vitriol flows from his pen… his gift is not for satire, but for comedy, and more especially comic characterization. It is the characters we remember. If Nicol, MacInnes, Grassick, Bonington and Whillans have never done anything else other than appear in Patey's songs they would still live on in our consciousness.

Apocryphal stories abound, celebrating Patey's ability to sing, drink and smoke the night away, barely closing his eyes for a couple of hours before dragging his exhausted companions off on some climbing sortie. Patey himself never seemed to be affected by drink, an attribute noticed by Joe Brown. 'Trying to match him drink for drink would be a good way for me to lose a day', he recalls. 'I remember lots of times going off to do routes in the Alps with my lips stuck to my gums with dehydration after a session on the whisky'. Brown also recalls Patey's phenomenal ability to travel enormous distances at any time of day or night: 'he never liked to stay and climb in the same area, so he'd drink in Aviemore and climb on the Ben or Torridon'. Brown also recalls, with some misgivings, Patey's eventual dependence on amphetamines.

I remember an argument once not long before he died, where he was violently against
the drugs that were becoming popular at the time. I think he realized the harm they
did because he had become a bit hooked.

Patey spent much of his National Service in the Marine Commando climbing unit.
It was a carefree life which he enjoyed, and he stayed in the Navy from 1957 till
1961. On his return to civilian life, Patey, now a married man (he married an
Aberdeen girl, Betty Davidson, in 1958), took on the large medical practice in the
Wester Ross town of Ullapool. His battered Skoda, tied together with bits of string
and cat-gut, was a familiar sight on the winding single track roads, either coming to
and from visits to his patients, or checking out the new-found paradise of climbing
potential on the crags and mountains that circled his new home. He thought
nothing of driving from Ullapool to North Wales for the weekend, where he would
sing, play his accordion all night and climb throughout the next day with abounding
energy. Tom enjoyed his job in Ullapool, and told Tom Weir he would rather be a
good doctor than a climber any day. He felt that climbing was hardly a reason for
living, but providing a good medical service to a remote region like Ullapool and the
North-West was vitally important.

It was during this time that Patey discovered sea-stacks, the long slender piles of
rock which grace the coastline of Scotland's north western seaboard. With Paul
Nunn, Brian Henderson and Brian Robertson he climbed the Old Man of Stoer, off
the coast near Lochinver, followed by Am Buachaille near Sandwood Bay with John
Cleare and Ian Clough before tackling the intimidating Old Man of Hoy on Orkney
with Chris Bonington and Rusty Baille. This outing formed the framework for the
BBC outdoor spectacular in 1969, which, for a short time at least, was to make the
climbers involved household names. Patey had a real love of climbing sea stacks and
Hamish MacInnes coined the nickname of Dr. Stack for him. Another climbing
contemporary, Sheffield based Paul Nunn, believes that Patey is probably best
remembered for his sea stack routes.

I think most climbers identify Tom Patey most clearly with stacks. They may be
unaware of his climbing in other areas, but they know him because of the Old Man of
Hoy. Although its a paradox that he soloed innumerable routes, he actually
orchestrated a lot of events and drew other people into them. The Old Man of Hoy

TV spectacular was really his idea and I would still argue that of all his climbs, that was the most important of all, both the first ascent and the television event.

Perhaps it was the magnetic power of television which causes Paul Nunn to hold such an opinion, for there is little doubt that in Scotland, Tom Patey is best remembered for his winter climbing. Along with others like Bill Brooker, Hamish MacInnes, Jimmy Marshall and Robin Smith, he pushed winter climbing standards during the fifties and sixties, particularly in the sphere of Scottish mixed climbing, using the style of his native Aberdeen school. Not to be outdone by all the new equipment designs which were being flaunted at the time, Hamish MacInnes recalls Patey inventing a pair of 'metal claws', rather like hand held crampons. 'They did not quite catch on', MacInnes comments wryly.

During the winter of 1968-69, Patey completed what was to be one of his last great winter routes, an awesome 8000 foot (2438 m) solo effort to complete the entire girdle traverse of the Coire Ardair face of Creag Meagaidh, that mastiff of a mountain which lies between Ben Nevis and the Cairngorms. Although not a technically difficult route, it has been described as a tremendous effort by an ingenious pioneer. Patey himself regarded it as one of his finest expeditions, although certainly not the most difficult.

Patey's interest was aroused by an article in a guide book which described '...a Girdle Traverse of the cliffs of Coire Ardair... is certainly the longest potential expedition of its kind in Great Britain... and still awaits its first complete ascent'. He tried to tempt Don Whillans into accompanying him. 'I don't get much excited about girdles', said Don gloomily, 'especially 8000 foot ones'. 'But it's perfectly simple', insisted Patey. 'You have two parties starting simultaneously from opposite ends, crossing over in the middle. The left-hand party led by a right-handed leader and the right-hand party by a left-handed leader'. 'Look mate', Whillans interrupted, 'Do you know what you want to do? You want to team up with a crab. It's got claws, walks sideways and it's got a thick head. This isn't a climb, it's a bloody crab-crawl!' And that became the name of the route.

Patey arrived in Coire Ardair with photographer John Cleare, London journalist Peter Gillman, and fellow Aberdeen climbers Jim MacArtney and Allen Fyffe. MacArtney's girl friend, Mary Anne Hudson came along too – it was her second winter route. Being comparatively late in the day, and realising that Cleare was planning to take photographs, Patey decided to solo alongside the climbers, 'A rope of five with a

MICK TIGHE, WHO CLIMBED THE OLD MAN OF STOER WITH PAUL
NUNN FOR THE FILM, ON THE TYROLEAN TRAVERSE THAT LEADS FROM
THE MAINLAND TO THE STACK.

leap-frogging snap-happy photographer is as mobile as a constipated caterpillar', he
wrote. But MacArtney and Fyffe were not pleased.

Even today, Allen Fyffe is convinced it was all premeditated; 'he set us up as camera
fodder – that was his intention all along'. By the time they reached the end of the first
pitch, Patey was out of sight. It was the last the rest of the team saw of Patey, although

MICK TIGHE, WHO DRESSED AS TOM PATEY FOR THE BBC TELEVISION RECONSTRUCTION
OF HIS ROUTE CRAB CRAWL ON CREAG MEAGAIDH. MICK IS HOLDING PATEY'S ORIGINAL
ICE HAMMER AND WEARING CONTEMPORARY SIXTIES CLOTHING.

he occasionally left encouraging arrows on the snow to show he had not forgotten it
was a team effort.

Patey's death, in May 1970, was described by Paul Nunn as 'one of those really non-
sensical things'. Nunn was one of a team of four; himself, Clive Rowland, Dave
Goodwin and Patey, intent on climbing a sea stack called The Maiden, off the
Sutherland coast a few miles from the mouth of Loch Eriboll.
Nunn recalls that:

> It was quite remote and difficult to get at... a long way off the shore, and the shore
> itself is about eight or nine miles from the road. We motored out for about four miles
> in a lobster boat and landed on the plinth at the bottom of the stack. The Maiden is
> actually two stacks – our route lay up the eastern one, and there was a fairly obvious
> narrow crack line going up the face. I led the first pitch, then Tom took over and

THE COBBLER, ARROCHAR ALPS. WITHIN EASY REACH OF GLASGOW, IT WAS THE FIRST MOUNTAIN CLIMBED BY W.H. MURRAY; IT WAS LATER THE SCENE OF MUCH EARLY ACTIVITY BY THE CREAGH DHU CLUB AND MORE RECENTLY WHERE DAVE CUTHBERTSON PUT UP THE ROUTE, WILD COUNTRY, IN 1979.

SMITH'S ROUTE, GARDYLOO BUTTRESS, BEN NEVIS. SET ON THE
DARK, IMPOSING NORTH EAST SIDE OF THE BEN THE ROUTE WAS
FIRST CLIMBED BY JIMMY MARSHALL AND ROBIN SMITH. TWO
DISTINGUISHED SCOTTISH CLIMBERS, ANDY NISBET AND
KEN CROCKET UNDERTOOK THIS ASCENT FOR THE CAMERAS.

PHOTOGRAPH: DAVE CUTHBERTSON

ABOVE: EASIER THAN IN MURRAY'S DAY. FILMING ON TOWER RIDGE,
BEN NEVIS – THOUGHT BY SOME TO BE MORE DIFFICULT THAN CLIMBING...
PILOT AND KEEN CLIMBER: DAVE CLEM.

LEFT: CRAB CRAWL, CREAG MEAGAIDH. THE 8500 FEET (2591 M) TRAVERSE
WITH THE CLIMBERS ON APPOLYON LEDGE GIVING A SENSE OF THE GRAND SCALE.

Photographs: Brian Hall, *far left*: Keith Partridge

ABOVE: CIOCH NOSE, SGURR A CHAORACHAIN, APPLECROSS. FIRST
CLIMBED BY CHRIS BONINGTON AND TOM PATEY IN 1960 AND DESCRIBED
BY TOM PATEY 'THE DIFF TO END ALL DIFFS', ALTHOUGH NOWADAYS
IT IS REGARDED AS A V. DIFF.

LEFT: EMERALD GULLY, BEINN DEARG. PAUL NUNN, BRIAN FULLER AND
TONY RILEY MADE THE FIRST ASCENT OF THIS CLASSIC LINE IN 1970.

ABOVE SHIELDAIG LOOKING NORTH TO THE TORRIDON MOUNTAINS.

reached the top – it was about 140 feet high. It was all very wobbly on the top, so I put in a few pegs and linked them together with slings to make an abseil. Clive went first, then Dave, then me and Tom came last. Fairly typically of Tom, he was wearing a big, baggy woollen jumper under his anorak. We saw him start his abseil. He went into space after about twenty feet and then he got down about another ten feet with about 100 feet still to go. Then he stopped. We could not see what the problem was and it was actually becoming a bit gloomy because the weather was getting bad. We could see him suddenly jerk a little bit on the rope and then suddenly he just fell off the rope altogether. He just fell through the air – bang, flat on his back on the plinth of the stack.

It was later discovered that Patey was using a karabiner which did not have a locking gate. It had somehow become caught in his clothing and as he jerked to try and free it the live rope opened the karabiner, came out, and Patey fell to his death. Nunn was the first to reach him but it was obvious he was dead. 'He had sustained very bad injuries to the back of his head and there was no sign of life at all. It was all so sudden – instantaneous, and we just could not believe it'.

What followed was a nightmare. Rising seas prevented the lobster boat from landing and the climbers had to jump into it from the plinth. It was a horrifying journey, with everyone bailing to keep water out of the boat. Eventually they landed, and had to find a telephone. When the rescue team arrived, mostly local policemen, Clive Rowland and Paul Nunn went back out with them, back into the horrendously high seas to collect the body. 'The whole thing left us numb for years,' says Nunn.

> I had been involved in a lot of accidents before, but not quite in the same way, not as intimately. I know that Dave did not climb much for four or five years. For all of us it was a very peculiar experience, an experience which made us very adult in the game. In spite of the fact that I had been climbing for years, I realized I had very naive, romantic notions about climbing, notions which were badly dented by Tom's death.

ANDY CUNNINGHAM SHOWING CAMERON McNEISH TERRACE CRACK,
ONE OF THE EASIER ROUTES AT ARDMAIR CRAGS.

THE FAR NORTH: THE LAST GREAT WILDERNESS

What makes a land? Is it the people, or the landscape itself? Or is it a combination of both, an intertwining of culture and history, with the very natural features which have shaped them. If so, what happens when you take the people from the land? You can never shrug aside the ghosts of yesterday. You cannot ignore the ancient shielings and the dry stone dykes, the runrigs and the gable wall still standing.

The far north of Scotland is said to be the last remaining wilderness in western Europe. It is a largely unpeopled land because of the cruelty and hardship which forced the highlanders away from their native glens, leaving it empty for deer and sheep. The primeval forests which once covered the land have been wiped out and the hills are bare. The shielings are no more. Today it is a land that attracts those who love wild places, with areas of stark mountains rising from the western sea.

Torridon is such an area. The main peaks of the area form a triptych of contrasting forms, each of which would be outstanding in any mountain area. First there is Beinn Eighe 3314 feet (1010 m) with its incredible Coire Mhic Fhearchair, whose Triple Buttresses offer some of the great climbing routes of the area. Then Liathach, 3458 feet (1054 m) whose pinnacled ridge tops steep slopes which have seen an explosion in winter climbing standards in recent years. Finally there is Beinn Alligin, 3235 feet (986 m), the jewel of Torridon with great natural cleft and amazing horns and some good winter gully climbing on the north-east face of Tom na Gruagaich.

LIATHACH, WHERE MANY OF THE BEST SCOTTISH CLIMBERS HAVE
PUT UP WINTER ROUTES IN RECENT YEARS.

North of Torridon, across the shimmering waters of Loch Maree stands Slioch 3219 feet (981 m) a magnificent prospect with a commanding presence. Beyond lie the great climbing crags of Creag Mhor Thollaidh and Carnmore, on the edge of the Great Wilderness, a vast area of wild, unspoilt land which boasts some of the most inaccessible Munros in the highlands: A'Mhaighdean 3173 feet (967 m), Ruadh Stac Mor 3015 feet (919 m), Beinn Tarsuinn 3071 feet (936 m), Mullach Coire Mhic Fhearchair 3327 feet (1014 m), Sgurr Ban 3196 feet (974 m), Beinn a'Chlaidheimh 3000 feet (914 m) and An Teallach 3484 feet (1062 m).

An Teallach is one of the most popular hills in Scotland on account of its high, airy ridge, taking in the eyries of Lord Berkeley's Seat and the Corrag Bhuidhe Buttresses. But the most incredible feature of An Teallach is her 1699 feet (518 m) deep corrie, Toll an Lochan, which compares in grandeur to Coire Mhic Fhearchair of Beinn Eighe.

Northwards, beyond Ullapool, lie four Munros – Ben More Assynt and Conival, Ben Klibreck and Ben Hope. Up here in the extreme north west lies a clutch of Scottish mountains which are grander than the vast majority of Munros, and all lie below that 3000 foot (914 m) plimsoll line. Ben More Coigach, Stac Pollaidh, Cul Mor and Cul Beag, Suilven, Canisp, Quinag, Arkle and Foinaven. This is all remote country, sequestered from the populous central belt of Scotland by distance, narrow winding roads, tales of man-eating midges and a reputation for fickle weather: an area considered best left for week-long holidays rather than weekend forays. Yet the Victorian pioneer mountaineers, often using the sea lochs for access, made their mark here.

In May 1882 two English climbers, Charles Pilkington and Horace Walker climbed a steep gully on the North West Buttress of Caisteal Liath on Suilven, reporting it to be of no great technical difficulty, but offering great exposure and insecurity. In 1906 the intrepid Dr and Mrs Inglis Clark climbed the West Buttress of Stac Pollaidh and the following year Harold Raeburn, climbed the Barrel Buttress of Sail Garbh on Quinag. G.T. Glover and Willie Ling climbed a long route on the First Dionard Buttress of Foinaven in May 1910 and later made a remarkable attempt on the Nose of Sgurr an Fhidhleir in Coigach.

Few other routes were climbed until after the Second World War, with the exception of a flurry of activity from Dr Jimmy Bell who climbed Bell's Gully and Eagle Buttress on Ben Hope with Duncan Myles in 1933 and later, with his wife, put up routes on Beinn Dearg and Cul Beag. In the fifties, Tom Weir, Len Lovat, Alec Smart and others explored the great quartzite crags of Creag Urbhard on Foinaven, and a host of new routes were climbed on Suilven, Stac Pollaidh and Cul Beag.

Compared to the other mountain areas of Scotland, the far north west remained relatively unexplored until fairly recently, and attracted a long, if fragmented, exploration by English raiders. Perhaps because the area is so remote the vast majority of Scottish climbers baulked at detailed exploration and have left the Sassenachs to get on with it. This is a tradition which has continued to the present day, with climbers like Paul Nunn, Clive Rowland, Martin Boyson, Doug Scott, Al Rouse, Brian Hall, Martin Moran and Mick Fowler making regular forays to check out and climb new routes.

In more recent years, the Scots have realized what a treasure they have in their northern domain, and development has been brisk with whole crags which were once virtually ignored, like Ardmair just north of Ullapool, now bristling with new lines. The long awaited publication of two, thick, guide books for the area by the SMC indicates the wealth of climbing that exists.

One English climber who has built up a long and lasting affinity with the north west is Paul Nunn. Nunn, President of the British Mountaineering Council, is a distinguished economic historian who lectures in Sheffield and has visited this area for many years, exploring its cliffs and corries in both summer and winter.

> We were attracted by the exploratory nature of the climbing. There were new things
> to do and very few climbers seemed to go there. Generally they were people we
> greatly respected, like Hamish MacInnes or Tom Patey. I think that psychologically
> the north west seemed almost as far away as Yosemite. But we were more interested in
> doing new things and we felt there was more scope for climbing new routes in the
> north west of Scotland than there was in California.

Like many of the climbers who regularly come up from the south to the north west, Nunn recognizes a certain similarity to Alpinism. He first went to the Alps in 1961, but had been in Scotland for a couple of years before that. His initial attraction to Scottish

PAUL NUNN, PRESIDENT OF THE BRITISH MOUNTAINEERING COUNCIL, AND
LONG-TIME DEVOTEE OF CLIMBING IN THE FAR NORTH.

winter climbing was twofold: firstly there was a great sense of achievement if you actually got up a route in what were often difficult, harsh weather conditions, and secondly he saw it as a form of Alpinism. He draws a parallel with the Victorian pioneers, many of whom were also Alpinists. He explains the point further:

> The routes are not quite as long as Alpine routes, but the days are short and there is an excitement in having to get up and go. Unless you're on the move pretty early you are not going to get anywhere, and that gives an impression of being in quasi-Alpine conditions. I think there is also a stark beauty about it that I really enjoy. It is as much to do with walking as climbing and there is the atmosphere of just being on snowy mountains.

Surprisingly, Nunn also admits that the fickleness of the highland weather can be appealing, and you learn to cope with conditions that are unpredictable.

> You can't just go out and climb in the Californian sun everyday… you've got to seize the day when it is right. That is true about British climbing in general and Scotland epitomizes that in the most extreme form. I do not think you would get far with Scottish climbing unless you were opportunistic. You would just go home, fed up with sitting around in cafés or pubs looking out at the terrible weather. I think that is what many people do not understand about Scottish climbing, and that is the importance of getting out there and putting your nose in front of the problem. You can miss superb opportunities by being pessimistic.

Another English climber who enjoys a reputation of being a supreme opportunist is Mick Fowler. His contribution to the development of winter climbing in the North West has been considerable, especially as, for years, much of his climbing on Scottish mountains was limited to weekend forays from his home in London. It was early in his climbing career that Fowler turned his attention to some of the great Scottish mountain crags, first of all trying a week in February for three years in a row, when interminable rain made him begin to wonder if he had thought out the best possible game plan. He then started driving to Scotland for weekends and soon discovered that his outings were infinitely more productive. Fowler's weekend dashes from his London Inland Revenue desk have passed into climbing mythology.

It was a routine many people would find bizarre: driving through a Friday evening, two hours' sleep in the back of the car, a hard day's climbing on Ben Nevis or in the Cairngorms, sleep in the car again, another day's climbing, another long drive on winter roads through the night, and back to the office bleary-eyed on Monday morning. It gave a whole new meaning to escaping from London for the weekend.

In essence, the distances involved, about 1200 miles (2000 km) for the round trip, are comparable with driving to the Alps every weekend. Fowler and his friends soon ticked off all the routes they wanted to climb on the popular mountain crags in Scotland, places like the Cairngorms, Glencoe and Ben Nevis, so they gradually travelled further afield, still on weekend dashes from London. It was not until 1985 that they started to realize the potential of the North West of Scotland, on those prehistoric mountains of Torridon, and even further north in Sutherland.

> I had not climbed up there before. I had spent some time on Skye and in terms of winter climbing there was very little known about these areas. It was very much a matter of finding your own way, and with nobody else on the crags at all, it was the perfect place for the adventurous climber.

It is this type of adventure climbing that characterizes Fowler, rather than the bolt-protected kind of climbing that is becoming popular in some areas of Scotland. He is against bolts, because he believes that they reduce climbs to an exercise.

> I know that becomes difficult when you consider an area like Malham in Yorkshire, and perhaps it is a valid argument that if bolts were not used there would be hardly any routes there, but to my mind we have to very careful that we preserve challenges for the future for those people who are good enough to do them, rather than just reduce the whole thing to a gymnastic exercise.

While Fowler's list of first ascents in the north west highlands includes brilliant mixed routes, like Gully of the Gods and Great Overhanging Gully on Beinn Bhan, he definitely has a preference for good obvious ice routes.

> I like there to be a line which basically means it is either a gully or a series of connected ice dribbles. I like to walk into a corrie and say 'Wow, I want to go and climb that'. That is far preferable to wandering up to the foot of a rock climb and having to get out the guide book to see exactly which groove you are supposed to be

MARTIN BURROWS-SMITH SEEN HERE ON NEART NAN GAIDHEAL (E5 6A), A
ROUTE FIRST CLIMBED IN 1989 BY ANDY CUNNINGHAM.

climbing. Torridon is one of the best areas in Britain. It is an area relatively
unfrequented by climbers and with magnificent scenery. I personally find it much
more inspiring than the Cairngorms. The north west has a climbing flavour of its
own, an atmosphere created by few people and superb scenery. There is a real feeling
of adventure, even today, once you get past Inverness and on to the single track
roads, especially when its just getting light after a twelve hour drive.

MICK FOWLER, A SUPREME OPPORTUNIST, HAS MADE A SUBSTANTIAL
CONTRIBUTION TO SCOTTISH WINTER CLIMBING.

It is this sense of distance and remoteness that appeals to Fowler. Despite the fact that a number of Scots, including Tom Patey, Philip Tranter, the very active leader of the Corriemulzie club, and Mick Geddes were all extremely active in the sixties, seventies and eighties, Fowler argues that the area has been comparatively neglected. He illustrates this by pointing out that Poacher's Fall in the north east coire of Liathach's Spidean a'Coire Leith, the most obvious ice fall in the North West, was not climbed until 1976, seventeen years after Point Five Gully on Ben Nevis.

> That is quite outrageous. Perhaps it sums up the general attitude that people had to the north west for a long, long time. That it was too far and too infrequently in condition to warrant going there. When I started coming up here I never met another climber. Then I would meet some people but I would know them all. But in the last four or five years it has become more popular.

This popularity has been reflected in the development of a number of small crags that, until the mid eighties, had been neglected. A good example are the crags at Ardmair, which are just north of Ullapool. While climbers have recognized the excellent climbing on northern crags like Stac Pollaidh, Sgurr an Fhidhleir or the sea cliffs at

Reiff, Ardmair Crags were neglected. Writing in *Climber Magazine* in 1990, Allen Fyffe suggested why Ardmair had been ignored for so long.

> Many climbers who drove north from Ullapool must have seen the profile of the
> Monster Buttress. Perhaps, like I did for many years, they assumed that anything so
> obvious and not climbed on must be poor rock or there would be routes on it.

The Ardmair Crags consist of several buttresses, all Torridonian sandstone and much of it is good quality rock. Most of the climbs follow deep, well defined cracks, and the most stunning feature of the crags, a vertical crack-line which runs out to a huge nose, has been climbed by Richard Mansfield, at E5 6b. This route, Burning Desire, is the hardest route on the crags, its crux being a bulging section of the crack, and not the overhanging nose above.

It was not until 1985 that two local climbers, Alex Taylor and Fraser Fotheringham, recorded the first route on the crags, Friends Retrieval, E1 5b. Between 1985 and 1989 a handful of other routes were added, and recorded in the SMC Journal. This publicity led to a concentrated burst of exploration by instructors from Glenmore Lodge with Allen Fyffe one of the instigators of this exploration. By the end of 1989 there were over seventy recorded routes, mostly in the HVS to E3 grades.

The lesson of Ardmair is that there are probably other equally stunning crags waiting to be developed. With the long awaited publication of the SMC guides to the Northern Highlands, there is a feeling among many traditionalists that the exploratory nature of the area will be spoiled, but with an area bigger than the whole of Wales – ninety nine percent of it uninhabited – and a coastline which stretches for hundreds of miles with all its indentations, there is surely still enough exploration to satisfy even the most intrepid. As many climbers have wryly noted, even with modern roads, it is still a long way from Glasgow and Edinburgh.

RAB ANDERSON ON THE FIRST ASCENT OF THE DEVIANT, COIRE AN LOCHAIN
IN THE NORTHERN CORRIES OF THE CAIRNGORMS.

AT THE LEADING EDGE:
THREE MODERN CLIMBERS

In this book we have explored some of the key names of twentieth-century Scottish mountaineering. With the continual development of climbing equipment, and with more and more climbers invading the highlands in search of new climbs, it is impossible to name any one climber and say he is the sport's leading figure. Today there is an elite group of climbers who are all at the leading edge of the sport.

Three of this group, all Scottish-born climbers, represent the various elements within modern Scottish mountaineering and whilst they are not unique (we are not, for example, claiming, that they are the best mountaineers of their time), they do represent the determination and the will to succeed that is undoubtedly a vital ingredient in modern climbing.

Edinburgh-born Rab Anderson is rather unusual in being in one of the few leading climbers who holds down a steady career, working in a housing agency. A classic example of Rab's winter climbing is Inclination, a modern mixed route graded at VII 8, in Coire nan Lochan in Glencoe. Climbers have always had a well-developed sense of irony when naming their latest triumph and Inclination is no exception to this rule.

When Rab, who introduced his partner Chris to this kind of climbing, and Rob Milne made their first attempt they found the route so steep that it was –impossible to see the line it took because the rock holds so little snow. It does not involve the traditional Scottish mixture of snow and ice climbing but a new technique which utilizes rock, frozen turf and the tiniest of ledges. It is on to these insecure platforms the climber places the point of a crampon and the very end of an ice axe pick and begins a delicate, complicated series of moves that include 'torquing' up on the axe to the next almost invisible hold.

Rob Milne wrote vividly about their route,

> The next pitch looked horrendous. After a sloping ledge, the climb goes up a thin
> crack splitting a vertical wall. The wall was devoid of snow, in spite of the good
> conditions. As I was about to learn, this was because it was vertical and had no
> ledges. Rab muttered something about this being an aid pitch in summer. To his
> knowledge, it had never been free-climbed, summer or winter. I could see why.

Rab is not simply a leading exponent of winter climbing, he is also active in summer
and has put up an impressive list of new routes from Ben Nevis to the Cairngorms.
Recently he has been making spectacular first ascents in Glencoe, adding routes of
difficulty alongside the old classics on Church Door Buttress, Bidean nam Bian and on
Garbh Beinn of Ardgour. He always has an eye open for a new line and once he has
seen a potential new route, he analyses its feasibility, develops first attempts on the
rock, continues with successive struggles up the vertical face and finally concludes with
a completed first ascent.

Sport climbing, or bolt climbing, uses pre-placed bolts drilled into the rock for protection and is still highly controversial among British climbers. Unlike virtually all traditional climbing, where the leader places the protection into the rock and where this
placing is part of a risk game, Rab Anderson has been an energetic champion of 'sport'
climbing. He justifies his controversial stance by arguing,

> Traditional climbing appeared to have reached a high point with a number of
> outstanding bold leads. There was nowhere to go for the leading climbers of the day.
> The sport had to progress – to sit still was to stagnate.

Sport climbing was originally developed from the French, and has its own discreet code
of ethics. This climbing sees the leading practitioners deliberately choose a route that
is often initially impossible to climb. A phenomenal amount of time, in many cases
upwards of twenty days, is then spent practising a number of separate moves that are
ultimately put together to form a complete ascent.

The aim of this type of climbing is to produce a 'clean' ascent, or to use the sport
climbers jargon, a red-point, in which the climber does not put any weight on the bolts
or slings placed as protection.

Rab Anderson explains:

> At some point you have to psyche up and go for it… a clean lead from bottom to top
> without weighting any of the gear. Not easy, and not the foregone conclusion you
> might imagine, especially if you're climbing at your limit. I failed to redpoint a route
> in France last year and just had to go back to do it and get it off my mind.

Rab Anderson argues that the physical risk of traditional climbing is replaced by a mental challenge. He also claims that climbing at this standard has another major problem: the human body cannot, in many cases, take such punishment and a range of potentially serious injuries to muscles and tendons are now common in this group of climbers. Anderson, once the traditionalist, has shocked many of his peers by championing this new form of climbing and believes 'that sport climbing and bolts are the best things that have happened in my climbing career'. For one with such an active climbing career it is worth reflecting on the significance of such a statement.

Another Scottish climber who has also embraced sport climbing is Dave Cuthbertson, and like Anderson, he comes from a strong traditionalist background. He started exploring the outdoors as a hill walker with the Boys Brigade, then progressed to indoor climbing with his school at Meadowbank Sports Centre in Edinburgh, and eventually to rock climbing with friends at weekends. One of those school friends was Rab Anderson.

Cubby, as he is universally known, has always been driven by a strong competitive streak but when he first went climbing he actually found the experience quite scary.

> I found it difficult and intimidating. But I soon wanted to climb better than those
> around me. I had a real urge to climb the hardest grades which were VS (very severe)
> at that time.

It did not take him long to realize that he had an natural aptitude for climbing and during his first day's climbing he managed a VS. He believes now, on reflection, that it was possibly a dangerous thing to do, but climbing had gripped him. It was not just the competition but also the adventure, particularly the opportunity to escape from a working-class Edinburgh background and see different places with like-minded companions, enjoying the camaraderie and the fun. It is that inherent competitive instinct that has kept Cuthbertson at the forefront of British climbing for twenty years and which naturally aroused in him an interest in competition and sport climbing. With the increasing fragmentation of mountaineering into various disciplines including hard rock climbing, winter mountaineering, Alpinism, Himalayan expeditions, competition climbing and sport climbing, Cubby felt a conflict with his natural desire to reach the highest levels in every aspect of the sport. So, in the last few years he has concentrated largely on sport climbing because it demands so much commitment in terms of training and climbing at the necessary high standard.

Cubby's personal challenge for the future is to pioneer a route at the highest Scottish standards, and he believes that a route he has been working on in Glen Nevis, near Fort William, will be at that high level.

> The climb, when you look at the cliff, might not actually look all that difficult because you can see the odd feature here and there. The climb is quite long, by sport climbing standards, about 80 feet, but as soon as you pull off the ground the climbing is on so many poor holds at a fairly high angle. There is a very hard section about half way up, and even if you manage to get past that, there are even more hard moves with some really strenuous moves right at the very top.

Completion of this route in Glen Nevis is at the top of Cubby's immediate agenda. He describes it simply as his 'project', but it is an objective which requires him to be in the very best physical and mental condition and results in an arduous training regime.

> I have to be satisfied that I am really being stretched to my limit and it is important to ensure that I have done something which has really challenged me. I now realize that often means that I have achieved something which is quite significant, not only in Scottish climbing, but in British terms or even in world class terms. But first and foremost it is definitely between me and the rock.

It is undoubtedly this competitive urge which has kept Cubby at the top end of the sport for some twenty years. There have been a host of young climbers who have appeared during that time, showing great promise, but who have then vanished from the scene. Cubby believes that his interest in climbing has been maintained first and foremost because he loves climbing, and has a drive to climb well.

A YOUNG DAVE CUTHBERTSON CLIMBING SPOCK (E2, 5C) ON THE EAST BUTTRESS
OF SRON NA CICHE, COIRE LAGAN, SKYE, IN THE EARLY EIGHTIES.

I have done something in the region of 300 new routes and there are some climbs which really stand out. I could go to a crag and do 100 new routes in the space of a couple of weeks, but that would not mean anything to me. What is important is to produce something which I think represents quality, is challenging and is breaking new ground. When I did Wild Country in 1979 on the Cobbler it was the first time where I felt I had used bouldering techniques on a climb – to climb to your absolute limit high on a mountain route and not just a couple of feet off the ground! I felt I had achieved something there, that I had let myself go and climbed to my limit.

Wild Country represented a breakthrough in Cubby's career and a huge step forward in Scottish climbing. That was followed by other important extreme routes including Revengeance on Aonach Dubh, in Glencoe, Romantic Reality and Gone with the Wind on Buachaille Etive Mor, and Requiem on Dumbarton Rock, which was probably the hardest rock route in the world at the time of its first free ascent in 1983. Yet it is another route, Prophet of Purism on Aonach Dubh, which stands out in Cubby's mind, largely because he climbed it on sight in traditional style.

I attempted Wild Country on sight, but failed because the rock was just too dirty to climb at such a high standard, so I had to abseil down and clean it up. I remember feeling guilty for having to do this. I could not get any more protection in, so what I did in the end was actually pre-place a line. That sort of thing was going on a lot at the time, and it was something that I was really against in Scotland.

While the indoor climbing walls of Britain report a booming trade, as young climbers, of both sexes, spend much of their winter training hard for sports climbing, twenty six year old Graeme Ettle chooses to ignore his peers and specialize in the less glamorous Scottish winter climbing scene. For the past four years Graeme has lived in Aviemore, spending as many days as he possibly can on the snow-bound crags and buttresses of Scotland's winter mountains. One of Graeme's concerns is that there are few climbers his age involved in top class winter climbing.

GRAEME ETTLE (LEFT) AND RAB ANDERSON EXTOLLING
THE JOYS OF SCOTTISH WINTER CLIMBING.

In a recent interview given in *Climber* magazine Graeme Ettle expanded on this theme:

> There are any number of climbers of my age climbing hard on indoor walls or on
> bolted routes, but very few are active at the highest levels during the winter. In areas
> such as Beinn Eighe, there are acres of climbable lines, all in the top grade, the
> equivalent of E3 routes and above in winter conditions. If more young climbers had as
> much commitment to winter climbing as they have to summer sport climbing, the
> result would be tremendous, but it is not happening. Wall climbing takes place in such
> a controlled environment that it is very hard to imagine anyone breaking away from it.
> If I am on a route and fail, then I am involved in hours of hassle before I reach safety.
> If you fail on a wall, you simply drop off and go home. Where is the comparison?

Yet winter climbing does exact special characteristics. Allen Fyffe has said that it is an
odd aspect of the sport to specialize in because the conditions are so fickle. You can wait
for weeks for routes to come into condition. Graeme Ettle finds its difficult to be precise
about what attracts him to this kind of climbing:

115

It is very hard to describe. Winter climbing in Scotland encompasses not only the skills of a rock climber but the skills of the all round mountaineer. In summer you just tend to trot off to your crag with a light rack, a couple of ropes, nice warm conditions and it's great fun. In winter, it is a much harsher environment, and the gear is a lot bulkier and more cumbersome. The hours actually spent climbing in winter are fairly restricted, not only to the hours of daylight, but also due to the amount of days of good weather which allow you to go climbing. Every day in winter is probably worth ten good days in summer, and this is why it takes an awful long time to build up a good skill level in winter. It is simply a much greater challenge.

Graeme Ettle's enthusiasm leaves you breathless as he bombards you with a mixture of forceful statement and self belief. He talks the same way as he climbs, fast, direct and with vigour and it would not be far off the mark to describe his love affair with climbing as obsessive. A similar obsession can also be found in his choice of Scotland as his favourite place for climbing:

A big day climbing in the Alps is hard, but in my experience it is nothing compared to hard days in Scotland. You can climb a lot harder in Scotland and there is an awful lot of very technical climbing too. For instance, there are one or two things I have done in the Cairngorms that have left me unable to walk for twenty four hours and pumped out for three days.

Graeme also gets immense satisfaction from just being among the mountains, enjoying a genuine pleasure from walking in and out to a climb. Living in Aviemore he has a particular affinity with the nearby Cairngorms and he probably spends about half of his time in these mountains.

The Northern Corries of the Cairngorms are basically my back garden. I can see them in the morning, I can see them in the evening – I know exactly what is happening up there with the weather and the conditions. I think it is a wonderful place to climb, especially in winter. The rest of the time I will climb in places like Beinn Eighe and Liathach in Torridon, and Glencoe. I like the remoteness of a lot of places, but I do not stomp off just for the seclusion. The quality of the route is very important to me and it's that quality that I am aiming for.

Graeme has made a conscious decision to sacrifice virtually everything for climbing.

When he began climbing he had a full time job and, like everyone else, went climbing at the weekends. More recently he has felt an urge to climb all the time and he suffers great frustration if he cannot climb either through bad weather, unsuitable conditions, or simply because he is laid low with a cold for a few days.

Unlike some other sports, it can be very hard to discern who the best climbers are at any one given time. In that sense climbing is not a directly competitive sport and Graeme Ettle is at pains to make clear that he does not necessarily consider himself to be at the top of his sport. He claims that he simply functions at a very active level, although he will admit to certain pressures to be the best.

> Those kind of things always haunt you. You should be better or you should climb the hardest route. Or, are you the best there is? But it does not really bother me a great deal. I think in climbing it is very hard to discern who is the best, or who is the top climber of the day. Winter climbing has so many different aspects to it, and there is such a wide range of difficult climbs around requiring different skills that you just could not pin down one person and say he is the best.
>
> Also, climbing is an extremely personal thing. Going onto untracked territory and doing something that has not been done before, and not knowing whether you are actually going to get to the top or not. With routes that have already been done, even at the hardest level, you know that they have been climbed before, that it is possible, and that takes a lot of the sting out of it.

GRAEME ETTLE LEADING THE FINGER CRACK ON THE CRUX OF WHITE MAGIC,
ALADDIN BUTTRESS, IN THE NORTHERN CORRIES.

NEW DIRECTIONS

Looking back through a hundred years of Scottish mountaineering it is clear that there have been definite peaks and troughs in the development of the sport. In all the peaks, but more importantly, in all the troughs, there have still been climbers on the hills enjoying themselves. The vast majority of these people will not have been challenging the prevailing standards nor creating new routes, but just accepting the challenge the mountains pose for them as individuals. Most climbers, then and now, do not worry whether the sport that we know as mountaineering is developing or stagnating. It is a personal game, and most of us take part in it, and love it, at that level.

In each decade, however, there are those at the top level, those at the peak of the performance pyramid, those who set new skill levels and push back the accepted levels of what is 'justifiable'. Today, that level is exceptionally high, whether on rock or on snow and ice, and to achieve it ambitious young climbers are specialising. Just as Graeme Ettle has committed himself to winter climbing, just as Dave Cuthbertson and Rab Anderson are spending more time on bolted sport routes, so many young climbers, male and female, are sticking to one particular facet of what we know generically as mountaineering. Whilst these new climbers show great levels of commitment, some would argue that their actions might not be in the best interests of Scottish climbing. Allen Fyffe, for example, suggests that Scotland is not really the best place to specialize.

Many of the good rock climbers in Scotland tend to end up going south, to Sheffield or the like. I can see now that modern rock climbing, and bolt climbing, is just totally separate from mountaineering. It is not the same thing at all. Similarly, you can have a really frustrating time if you want to specialize in winter climbing – you can spend weeks, even months, when there is not much doing. To get the best out of Scotland you have to be an opportunist. You need to take what is going when you can.

Of course, most of the climbers from previous generations perfectly fit Fyffe's description, being accomplished all-rounders who always grasped the opportunities when they could, in summer or in winter. But there is a danger in looking backwards when trying to assess the future. Things are different nowadays from, for example, Jimmy Marshall's day in the late fifties and sixties when one of the chief motivations was still the exploratory nature of the climbing. In fact, Marshall firmly believes climbing is going downhill in terms of enjoyment.

> Apart from the few people climbing at the forefront and the height of their skills, we must acknowledge that the mass of people in the mountains must be deprived of that exploration. It is not even a tick-the-guide-book mentality, it is just that everything today is exposed and people are not allowed to do things for themselves. If you go to the hills as a youngster of fifteen or sixteen and you are ill clad and end up being rescued from the wrong glen you are accused of being reckless! Yet that is the very mould in which we went to the hills. We were badly clad and had no knowledge of where one glen went from the other or what it looked like. We relied on finding precious wee notes of information, but now the information about things is printed so fast that I think it deprives the masses of that adventurous quality of mountaineering.

Yet Jimmy Marshall does not look to the future of Scottish climbing with pessimism.

> I am not depressed by what has happened. I just feel sorry for the young folk that they have missed such an era. I still go crazy as I recall the pleasure and wildness of mountains. It is so enriching but I do regret that today you never see kids out on the hills unless they are wearing anoraks and proper boots and there is somebody organising it and directing them.

While that may be true of the more formal introductions to mountaineering, through outdoor centres or Youth Clubs where governing bodies insist that leaders and instructors have at least a basic minimum leadership qualification, there are still many people, not just the young, finding their own way onto the mountains, attracted by those elements of enrichment that attracted the climbers of yesteryear. The main difference now is that the hills are no longer unpeopled as they were in Murray's day. Even on a quiet weekend in Glencoe or Ben Nevis there will be hundreds of climbers heading for the crags – many climbing at a very high standard and even attempting new routes.

During the filming of the television series which accompanies this book it was fascinating to watch some of the climbers involved pointing out new lines and possible new routes, even in popular places like Creag Meagaidh, Ben Nevis and the Northern Corries of the Cairngorms. It is equally fascinating to realize that an area such as Ardmair Crags, north of Ullapool and only ten minutes walk from the main road, should have lain undeveloped for so many years. Clearly there are still ample opportunities for younger climbers to make their mark on the Scottish scene, as Graeme Ettle readily admits,

> There is a vast amount of new routes still to be climbed. Every decade that goes by sees new skills and techniques being developed, new gear, new attitudes and new inspirations for doing routes, and Scotland is a very, very big country. People say that certain places have been climbed out, all the routes have been done and there are no natural lines left. I think that is a very blinkered attitude and in the next ten years people will realize that there is a lot to be done, especially in the more remote areas. Possibly in some of the easier areas a lot seems to have been done, but I think even that could change.

Perhaps in twenty or thirty years' time we will recognize the nineties as being a time of change and development. Allen Fyffe is optimistic about the future,

> I think that there is still room for everybody if it is handled the right way. When people start to become fanatical about their own point of view that is when you get problems over bolting, or sport climbing or whatever…

But one thing is certain: no matter how many youngsters take up sport climbing on low-lying crags, no matter how many climbers become involved in the strict training and discipline of competition climbing, there will always be people testing themselves not against the crag or ice-filled gullies, but against themselves. That is where the spirit of mountaineering lies, exactly where it has lain for the last hundred years.

THE CLIMBERS

Norman Collie Victorian pioneer of world-wide importance, Collie is best remembered for two climbing discoveries made with his friend and guide, John Mackenzie: Sgurr Alasdair, the highest peak in the Black Cuillin and the huge tower of rock on Sron na Ciche, which Collie named The Cioch.

Harold Raeburn Remarkable for the advanced technical nature of his climbing, there are numerous routes throughout Scotland which bear his name. Many of his first ascents were made solo including Observatory Ridge (1901) and Observatory Buttress (1902) on Ben Nevis. Later climbs were so far ahead of their time that they went unrepeated for a quarter of a century.

W.H. Murray In the 1930s, Murray re-discovered the Scottish mountains with a freshness of the early pioneers. This is reflected in the book he later wrote as a prisoner of war, *Mountaineering in Scotland*. One of his first ascents was the winter route on Garrick's Shelf, Buachaille Etive Mor (1937).

Jimmy Marshall Perhaps the single most important figure in post-war Scottish climbing, Marshall has an impressive list of first ascents including Trapeze (1960), a complex rock route up the massive east buttress of Aonach Dubh in Glencoe. Robin Smith (*see below*) nicknamed him 'The Old Man' and was encouraged by Marshall, as were climbers like Dougal Haston, Jimmy Stenhouse and J. Moriarty.

Robin Smith Climber with strong impact on both summer and winter climbing in Scotland out of all proportion to the shortness of his life. From The Bat on Carn Dearg Buttress, Ben Nevis (1959), described as the hardest rock climbing route at the time in Britain, to The Needle on the Shelter Stone Crag, Cairngorms, which he climbed in the year of his death in 1962.

Dougal Haston Probably best remembered for the first British ascent of Everest with Doug Scot. But his climbing and writing career both started in Scotland. Besides The Bat, some of his best Scottish routes include Hee Haw, Aonach Dubh, Glencoe (1959), Kneepad (1959), Gearr Aonach, Glencoe, The Big Ride (1964), Etive Slabs, Beinn Trilleachan, and Inbred (1964), Creag Dubh.

Tom Patey Charismatic and prolific climber, Patey's name is closely linked with sea-stacks like The Old Man of Hoy (1966). His death in 1970 occurred on the descent after a successful first ascent of another sea-stack, The Maiden. Between 1955 and 1969 he made numerous first ascents in winter on Creag Meagaidh, and in 1969 completed the massive 8500 foot (2590 m) solo traverse of the mountain, entitled Crab Crawl.

Paul Nunn President of the British Mountaineering Council, Nunn has made an impact on the exploration of the Northern Highlands, with many first ascents like Millennium, Foinaven (1982). Nunn also joined Patey in his sea-stack exploits and was with Patey when that climber died abseiling.

Mike Fowler Significant contributor to winter climbing in the Northern Highlands, where his list of first ascents includes brilliant mixed routes like Gully of the Gods (1983) and Great Overhanging Gully (1984), both on Beinn Bhan.

Allen Fyffe A member of the Aberdeen school, Fyffe has been extremely active in Scottish climbing for over twenty five years. His major Cairngorm routes include King Rat (1968) and Black Mamba (1969) on Creag an Dubh Loch. As an instructor at Glenmore Lodge, he helped develop unfashionable crags like Cairn Etchachan.

Rab Anderson climbs at a high level in both summer and winter. Bold winter routes include Neanderthal (1987) on Bidean nam Bian,

Glencoe. Originally a traditionalist, Anderson is now a keen proponent of sport climbing seeing it as a way to enable climbers to develop the skill and stamina to push traditional standards even further.

Dave Cuthbertson is arguably Scotland's finest all-round climber who excels in extreme winter and summer climbing. He made the first winter ascent of Guerdon Grooves (1984), Slime Wall, Glencoe: no further ascent was attempted for over ten years. Like Anderson he has begun to specialize in the new area of sport climbing.

Graeme Ettle is a prolific and uncompromising climber with a special preference for winter routes. In the Cairngorms and Northern Highlands he has forged routes like The Independent Pineapple (1991), and The Third Wish on Aladdin's Buttress (1993), Coire an t-Sneachda.

FURTHER READING

THE FOLLOWING SELECTION ECHOES MANY OF THE THEMES IN OUR TELEVISION PROGRAMME AND BOOK:

The Scottish Mountaineering Club Journal (SMCJ) has been published continuously since 1890 and is an outstanding reference source on all aspects of Scottish climbing. Many key climbers first published their essays within its pages and you can chart much of the development of Scottish climbing from it. A selection of the most influential articles from the SMCJ has been edited by W.D. Brooker in *A Century of Scottish Mountaineering*, (Scottish Mountaineering Trust, 1988).

The Scottish Mountaineering Club has also, since the early years of this century, published a number of *District Guides* to Scotland's mountains together with specialist *Climbing Guides*. Recently both series have been thoroughly revised and now appear in editions with many colour photographs.

TITLES IN THIS CLIMBING GUIDE SERIES INCLUDE:
Arran, Arrochar & Southern Highlands, Crocket & Walker (SMT 1989).
Ben Nevis, ed. Everett (SMT 1994).
Cairngorms Rock & Ice Climbs, Fyffe & Nisbet (SMT 1985).
Glencoe & Glen Etive, ed. Everett (SMT 1992).
Lochaber & Badenoch, Stead & Marshall (SMT 1981).
Northern Highlands, (2 vols.) ed. Everett (SMT 1993).
Skye: Rock & Ice Guide, Mackenzie (SMT 1982).

OTHER GUIDES INCLUDE:
Scottish New Routes, Anderson & Latter (Anderson & Latter 1986); (*Supplement* 1988).
Rock Climbing in Scotland, Howett (Constable 1990).
Winter Climbs, Ben Nevis and Glencoe, Kimber (Cicerone Press 1991).
Scottish Climbs, MacInnes (Constable 1971).

OTHER RELEVANT CLIMBING BOOKS INCLUDE:
Bell's Scottish Climbs, Bell (Gollancz 1988).
Ben Nevis, Britain's Highest Mountain, Crocket (SMT 1986).
Norman Collie, A Life in Two Worlds, Mill (Aberdeen University Press 1987).
Mountaineering in Scotland, Murray (Dent 1947).
Undiscovered Scotland, Murray (Dent 1951).
(A compilation of these two Murray titles is published by Diadem Books in 1979.)
Scotland's Mountains, Murray (SMC Guide 1987).
One Man's Mountains, Patey (Gollancz 1989).
Mountaineering Art, Raeburn (Fisher Unwin 1920).
Climbing in the Himalaya and other Mountain Ranges, Collie J.N. (David Douglas, Edinburgh 1902).
Tight Rope!, Gray D. (The Ernest Press 1993).

IMPORTANT ESSAYS ON SCOTTISH CLIMBING ARE IN:
Classic Rock, ed. Wilson (Diadem 1989); *Hard Rock*, ed. Wilson (Diadem 1992); *Extreme Rock*, ed. Wilson & Newman (Diadem 1987); *Mirrors in the Cliffs*, ed. Perrin (Diadem 1983); *The Games Climbers Play*, ed. Wilson (Diadem 1978).

How Climbing Routes are Graded

The routes undertaken by climbers have traditionally been graded, but with the increasing difficulty of modern climbs the system has become somewhat convoluted. The grades are divided between summer rock climbing and winter snow-and-ice routes. Climbers tend to assess one route against others they have climbed, but the following routes, which we filmed for the television programmes, do give some indication of how the grading system works in practice.

Rock climbing grades are:
Easy: no more than a good scramble.
Moderate (Mod): Collie's Route on the Cioch falls into this category.
Difficult (Diff): examples of this grade include Tower Ridge on Ben Nevis in summer conditions.
Very Difficult (V. Diff): Cioch Nose, Sgurr a'Chaorachain was given this grade after Patey and Bonington's ascent.
Severe (S) / **Very Severe** (VS): the sea-stack, Old Man of Stoer is a good illustration of a VS.
Hard Very Severe (HVS): for instance, Bludger's Revelation, Buachaille Etive Mor, Glencoe first climbed by Jimmy Marshall.
Extremely Severe (E) This grade has, over the years, spawned a numbers of sub-divisions that now extend to E7 – E8.

To make matters even more complicated for the outsider technical grades can be given to the hardest moves of VS and above, and the range is normally: VS – 4b, 4c, 5a; HVS – 4c, 5a, 5b; E1 – 5a, 5b, 5c; E2 – 5b, 5c, 6a; E3 – 5c, 6a; E4 – 5c, 6a, 6b; E5 – 6a, 6b. To give just two instances of this grade: Joanna George climbed First Wave, on Wave Buttress, Glen Nevis and Allen Fyffe and Andy Cunningham were seen on Primitive Dance at Ardmair Crags both are graded at E2. Dave Cuthbertson's new route in Glen Nevis is a bolted route and has, therefore, been graded using a French system for sport climbing. Cubby has given it a grading of 8c+ and claims it is the hardest route of its type in Scotland. Contrary to the impression given by some climbing magazines not everyone is climbing at E5 or above!

Winter routes are accorded a grade between I and VII but these gradings are only a general indication and a route may feel quite different to a climber according to the snow conditions prevailing at the time.
The current SMC guidebooks make the following distinctions:
Grade I: indicates simple snow climbs, with perhaps a corniced exit.
Grade II: includes gullies with either individual or minor pitches, or high angled snow with difficult cornice exits, and the easier buttresses under winter conditions.
Grade III: incorporates gullies which contain ice or mixed pitches; there will normally be at least one substantial pitch and possibly several lesser ones; also sustained buttress climbs without great technical difficulty.
Grade IV: gullies may include nearly vertical ice sections, while the buttresses will require a good repertoire of techniques.
Grade V: climbs are difficult, sustained and/or serious. Some may be well protected but technically very hard.
Grade VI and **VII**: routes have exceptional overall difficulties. The roman numeral indicates the overall difficulty of the climb; any accompanying arabic numeral represents the technical difficulty of the hardest sections of climbing. The aim is to grade modern mixed routes to indicate their high levels of technical difficulty, jointly with the frequently greater seriousness of the older-style ice routes. Smith's Route on Gardyloo Buttress, merits V, 5, which makes Marshall and Smith's original achievement all the more impressive.

GLOSSARY

Aneroid barometer: an instrument for measuring atmospheric pressure and from which heights may then be calculated.

Alpine-style climbing: originally used to describe a style of climbing in the Alps where the party moves simultaneously, travelling roped together over easier ground.

Arete: a sharp ridge.

Belay: a method of providing protection against the effects of a fall by one of the party.

Bolts: usually stainless steel, placed into a hole drilled into the rock to provide protection for climbers.

Bouldering: the climbing of small rocks ('boulders') in order to practice certain moves and tackle technical 'problems' – normally undertaken solo and without the use of a rope.

Chimney: a vertical fissure in the rock up which it is possible to climb.

Cornice: a consolidated body of snow, often unstable, overhanging a ridge or plateau.

Corrie: or coire, or cirque, is a steep-sided hollow high in the mountains.

Couloir: originally from French climbing and meaning an open gully.

Crampons: metal frames with spikes that are attached to boots to give a grip in winter especially on ice.

Front pointing: a technique developed using two projecting spikes at the front of crampons to grip into vertical ice.

Gendarmes: a projecting rock pinnacle on a ridge.

Howff: a rough shelter, often under rocks.

Ice-climbing: the climbing of frozen ice which has consolidated to form a vertical route.

Kletterschuhs: an earlier form of rock climbing boot.

Lochan: a small loch or lake.

Manse: the house of a Church minister in Scotland.

Mixed climbs: a winter route involving both snow and/or ice climbing together with some rock climbing.

Pitch: the climbing distance between two belay points.

Piton: a metal peg hammered into a crack in the rock.

Red point: one method of successfully leading a sport climbing route, in this case with the use of pre-placed karabiners.

Run-out: the length of rope between the leader and the second person.

Single rope tension: a technique used in tension climbing where the rope is used solely for protection.

Spindrift: loose snow blown by the wind.

Sport climbing: climbing using bolts where the skill is of a gymnastic and technical nature rather than of risk.

Tension climbing: often called aid or artificial climbing and where pitons, bolts and other equipment are used by the climber.

Torquing: a technique used on modern, hard mixed climbs. The pick of the ice-axe is placed into a crack and then is 'torqued' round to gain enough pressure for the climber to pull up on the axe without it popping out.

Tricounis: a type of nail hammered into the sole of a climbing boot and designed to provide a better grip on the rock.

Verglas: thin ice on rocks which makes climbing difficult.

Vibram: specially designed rubber soles for climbing boots.

INDEX

Page numbers in **bold** denote chapter devoted to subject. Page numbers in *italics* refer to illustrations.

PICTURE CREDITS

Rab Anderson: *113*.
John Cleare: *65, 87*.
J.N. Collie, Alpine Club Library: *24, 28, 30*.
Dave Cuthbertson: *56, 95, 102, 118*.
Richard Else: *59, 96, 115*.
Allen Fyffe: *105*.
Brian Hall: *46, 98*.
John MacEwen: *55*.
Cameron McNeish: *60, 78*.
Jimmy Marshall: *71*.
Keith Partridge: *57, 100, 106*.
Tom Prentice: *108*.
St Andrews University Photographic Collection: *38*.
Scottish Mountaineering Club Collection: *27, 36, 44-45*. Jimmy Marshall/ SMC: *68, 77, 81, 82*. Niall Ritchie/ SMC: *2, 7, 8, 12, 16, 84*.
University College, London: *20, 23*.
John Wilson: *49*.

Authors' acknowledgement

While every effort has been made to indicate the publishers of the books that have been quoted from in *The Edge*, in some instances this has not been possible. The authors would like to thank all those concerned and apologize for any omissions. (See also *Further Reading* p. 123.)